Am I Mad or What?

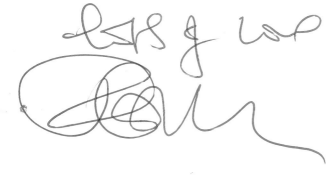

To Brian +
Gladys.

Pauline Carville

First published in Northern Ireland in 2022
by Excalibur Press

ISBN: 978-1-910728-61-1

Formatting & layout by
Excalibur Press

Cover design by
Oranga Creative

Excalibur Press
Belfast, Northern Ireland

team@excaliburpress.co.uk

07982628911 | @ExcaliburPress

excaliburpress.co.uk

This book was supported by the Arts Council of Northern Ireland

DEDICATION

I dedicate this book to My Mummy who supported and guided me through to recovery after returning home from London and My Daddy who has always watched over me and been someone to talk to in my darkest hours. I know you are both with me everyday and want you to know that I am so grateful and I love you. xx

Foreward

I would like to thank

The Psychotherapist - You know who you are!

My dear friend and Spiritual Life Coach Cynthia who has been with me on this long journey of recovery. You are such a great friend and Mentor and I am so grateful and appreciative for your guidance, understanding and of course your patient ear!

To my family who have given me great memories and stories and the love and support that I needed throughout.

To my publisher Tina Calder & Excalibur Press who set the seed of turning my 2011 Play "Am I Mad Or What" into a book and her encouragement for the other books that are still to come. You have gone above and beyond.

A very special and heartfelt thanks to my husband Robin Elliot who not only had to listen to me talk about writing this book for many years, I am so grateful for his shoulder that I have cried on throughout this process and of course for his fabulous interviewing skills which brought out all these stories that were sometimes embedded deep in my head. You really have been by my side since we met and throughout this sometimes extremely emotional journey. I couldn't have done it without you. xx

I would like to thank you the reader who identifies with Depression and hope that if you take anything from my experiences that it may be the realisation that you need help. Please don't hide it like I did.

For the readers that don't recognise Depression be thankful as I am for you as I wouldn't wish it on my worst enemy.

Finally I just want to say that I began writing this book to put the pain of the past behind me so that I could move on.

So if you have been like me and find it difficult to move on from the pain of your past? I urge you to put pen to paper and just get it out of your head. It is extremely therapeutic and it really does what the song says "Let It Go"

THE CLOUDS & ME

Light, dark, severe, heavy, clouds hang over me
Will they ever leave me? I don't know
I can't see anything like I use to
What's happened to me?

Every day I wake, my mind is so weary
Tired of the heaviness the clouds bring
I shower, hoping it will release the tension
Of the anxiety I feel.

I can't see through the clouds
I feel heavy and tired
My mind goes in circles
If you have a worry, sure give it to me
I will worry for you

My arms and legs have pins and needles
The physical repercussion of the clouds
Will I ever see clearly again
Will these feelings ever end?

Uncontrollable tears fall
Until my eyes hurt and feel heavy
All I want to do is sleep – maybe forever
My mind turns around so fast
My spinning mind,
I want to bash against the wall;

Will I ever see clearly again?
Or is this how life is supposed to be for me?

I sit on the chair staring at the wall
Time seems to go so slow
Yet I look at the clock and 8 hours have passed
Why me? Why?
How can life be so … Cloudy?

Doctors prescribe the meds required
Instead of relief, there is a diagnosis
Clouds get darker and thicker
Eyes get heavier and life seems duller
Sleeping is the only way to relieve this misery

My mind says drive into the Thames
My heart says no, my family
My head says take the pills to help you sleep
Only take more to sleep longer
But what if I don't wake?
So What!

PROLOGUE

Sitting in the Psychotherapist's office once again … in therapy.

By this time I had done my research. I was looking for someone who really could delve into my life and help me to break down the walls that I had built around me for protection, so high that even I couldn't work out what was going on behind them.

By now I had spent thousands of pounds on counsellors and therapists who always seemed to take the textbook option of what was causing the depression (what became known to me as 'the clouds' for over thirty years.

I was now extremely frustrated because no one had been able to help me to date in talk therapy, even though I was now much better than I had been in the early days of the diagnosis. I had now been medicated on Seroxat for the last fifteen years and I still felt like I hadn't gotten to the bottom of my condition. Why was I still feeling so unwell … mentally! So how was I going to live a normal life, without antidepressants if I still didn't know what had actually caused it?

I had tried numerous times to come off the medication, only to relapse into a deeper depression through withdrawal.

So here I was in a room with a Psychotherapist. He had been recommended to me by a friend who had suffered an episode of depression and he had been successful in his therapy journey.

What did I have to lose? How was this therapist going to help me that was different from the others? So I asked …

"What is the difference between a Psychotherapist and a Counsellor?

"A Counsellor works at a more immediate level, focusing on a current issue that is affecting the client. A Psychotherapist works and thinks at a deeper level and considers how the structure of the client's personality and emotional history affects their current experience"

He also explained that he had achieved his qualifications and training in Counselling as well as Psychotherapist, making him a highly qualified therapist.

Well, clearly my problem was complex as no one to date had been successful.

I knew now I was in the right hands! More importantly, I already trusted him!

Chapter 1 - Who Am I?

I just can not believe that I am here … again!

I haven't felt myself for years. So much so, I could say that I have lived longer feeling unwell than I have been well. How can this be? I used to be such a jolly person with such a positive outlook on life and over the years I have had to fight to feel good about myself and my place in this world, in this life.

The more I felt unwell in myself, the more I put myself into situations that have made me feel mentally unstable, unconfident, anxious, taking me further and deeper into this miserable existence that I have been living for longer than I can remember.

Sometimes I don't know who to be?

When I am my genuine real self either I get trampled upon or taken advantage of. If I play hard and speak hard, I can't cope with the reactions of others. If I try to be someone completely different then I know I'm acting and then I don't know who the hell I am. I think to myself. Am I mad or what?

That's probably why I love acting because I know the emotions that I am using, I am in control of. But the day to day feelings I can't control and all I feel is mixed up and confused. Some people can be so hard you know they like to play on your vulnerabilities.

For years I have made the wrong decisions about everything including friendships, finances and of course men. I just want to be like I used to be, full of plans and dreams that I believed in. Now I feel like nothing!

That's when the Psychotherapist began.

"Why don't you start at the beginning"

CHAPTER 2 - I DREAMED A DREAM

My big dream was to become a successful actor and singer where I was performing on the West End in both straight plays and musicals including T.V. and film.

My Mummy, sisters and I used to be glued to the television on a Saturday afternoon. I remember we started with the serious melodrama of "What Ever Happened to Baby Jane" and I was always fascinated by the incredible performances by Joan Crawford and of course my favourite Bette Davis.

I couldn't believe how hooked I was, by the depth of her emotional connection so much so, that I felt like it was real life. This is how real Bette's acting was, her eyes were so incredibly expressive. We also watched the old Western films and I was fascinated by John Wayne and Maureen O'Hara in the Quiet Man and couldn't believe that it was actually set here in Ireland. (But that's another story for later) This was my first taste of great acting and I felt a strong connection to being able to express emotions so true and real that this was the beginning of my desire to become an actor.

Saturday afternoons were also about the musical films and I then became not only hooked on the drama of those classic movies of the 1930's, but now we were watching the brightly coloured, sensational musical films of the 1950's with Doris Day, Frank Sinatra and Judy Garland. I now loved the combination of the real acting integrated with the singing. We would all have so much fun watching the shows with the dramatic ballads and the fun up-tempo numbers that we all sang along to. They were also so romantic which was another first feeling for me - of what I thought love would be like.

The feelings that I would get from watching these different styles of movies made me want to be able to do that. I was a deep thinker anyway so I connected to all those movies both the deep serious and the musical. My desire to be a singer came from watching the musicals and singing along to the characters in these movies.

Although I was singing before I could talk (as in the Abba song) but believe it or not I used to sing country songs. Although mummy watched the old movies and musicals her love of country music was shared with my daddy.

They loved Philomena Begley, Susan McCann and Margo, so my first singing gigs were in our living room in front of my mummy and daddy, brothers and sisters singing "Behind the Footlights" by Margo. I loved singing songs that would get a reaction from my mummy and daddy. I was pretty smart that I chose songs that they would like. Well that is where it all starts isn't it, that is your first audience? My mummy and daddy soon realised that I had something so they invited other family and friends over to hear me on a Saturday night Carville Soiree. Around this time I also remember running up and down Templetown Beach singing "The Hills Are Alive with the Sound of Music"

Before my discovery of country music, great classic movies and musicals I used to put on performances in our back garden. Actually I think I made a lot of enemies when I was about age eight or nine because I used to direct my friends in dance routines to all the coke a cola ads.

"Coke is it, the most refreshing way, to make the most of everyday and wherever you go and whatever you do there's something here waiting for me and you – Coke is it, coke a cola is it!

And the wee girl down the street used to get it wrong and I would scream …

"No! That's not right!" and I would direct it and redirect it and then direct it again. I mean we would do all these mad moves to songs from 'Fame' and 'FlashDance' with lifts and everything. We would even do these routines in roller boots. I was very creative in everything I did even then and because I loved it so much and it made me happy I would come up with new ways and opportunities to perform even if it was just for ourselves. That was enough!

While all this creativity was taking place I was living in West Belfast during the troubles. The fun, happy me making up dances and performing was a way for me to shut out what was also going on around me. As a child there was always a fear in the air. I felt that. There were things you weren't allowed to talk about or do. For example if anyone was outside the church make sure you don't sign anything, just walk on past. (The fear was that you may be signing up to be involved in something you couldn't take back). I would hear the bin lids being banged on the ground by the women going up and down the street.

We were well protected where I lived because there wasn't a lot of trouble round our way; however when the woman with bin lids came down our street that meant trouble was on its way. It wasn't as if we were living in the Lower Falls somewhere, we were living at the very top of the road and I always laugh and wind our Deirdre up because her and Geraldine were born in Turf Lodge and hung about the Lower Falls. I was born up at the top of the road and I would tell her that the rest of us including our Michael and Brendan were posh compared to her and Geraldine because of that.

We lived in Brooke Close just off Blacks Road and our house was the last house in a row of terrace houses in a little cul-de-sac. We were at the cul-de-sac end of the street which was really private with a back and side garden. We were lucky we could travel down LadyBrooke, through Andersonstown and Falls Road on the red city buses into the town or we could walk up the Brooke Drive hill onto Blacks Road and get the Blue UlsterBus into the city. This became handy when there were bomb scares or car hijacking on the Falls Road. Although I think most of us loved the red City Buses as they used square bus tickets that you put into a little machine and it would stamp your ticket. This was the teenagers dream, free bus rides as teens were very clever and would buy a bus ticket, rub candle wax onto each journey strip and double ding. Each time you rubbed off the wax to remove the stamp and there you started the candle process again. This was how most of my friends who went to St. Louise's or St. Dominic's travelled to school and were able to travel to the clubs in town when they were in sixth year. They saved a fortune. Did you do that? … Come on, admit it!

We were on the peace line that originally had a river between one side and the other. In the early days I remember our neighbours from both sides of the fence and although I was born when the troubles had already started, the people who lived across the barricades continued being neighbourly until the tensions became stronger as the years went on. Eventually we suffered attacks from across the river with stones and bricks and regularly had our windows smashed. My parents loved our house and the area and they knew that the rioting was from a select few and were not willing to be intimidated out of our home.

Singer songwriter Joby Fox lived on our street, although it was only later on that I discovered that. He was the first big success coming out of Belfast that I knew of. Joby was going off to London to sign a big record deal with Bap Kennedy and their band, the hugely successful Energy Orchard. Joby wrote their big hit 'Belfast'! Then years later Joby would sing at my wedding.

My family didn't have any connection to show biz, although my Daddy played the mouth organ at family do's. He would also sing in the Cooley Mountains "Oh These Are My Mountains and I'm Going home" That was him just expressing himself and the love of the Cooley Mountains " in the same way Mummy would cook the dinner belting out, Joe Dolan hits including 'It's You, It's You, It's You'. After all "There's No Show like a Joe Show".

After mummy and daddy realised I could sing they were really supportive. Don't get me wrong it's not like today where the kids have so many opportunities to get out there and perform. There weren't many options for a budding singer where I lived so when a talent competition in my school came up my friends and teacher at St. Anne's Primary School persuaded me to enter with my singing and my mummy and daddy said they would come. For me this was a really big deal at the time and I decided to sing my usual party piece 'Behind the Footlights'.

I won the competition and became really popular in school and my friend up the street in Brooke Drive and her Mummy would tell my parents that I had a really unique mature voice for my age and they thought I was great. (They are still big fans today) as well as my Primary Seven school teacher Mr Cullen. They advised my mummy and daddy to encourage me to keep singing.

I'm not sure whose idea it was for me to go to sing at the working men's clubs all over Belfast. Daddy drove me everywhere to sing, even to east Belfast which at that time was dodgy considering where I was from.

Nothing was going to stop me having the opportunity to perform. So my parents were behind me all the way and considering they knew nothing about show business they just knew that I was different and wanted to make sure I got what I needed in terms of opportunities

Daddy was so proud of my singing and he was more than happy to be driving me around the country after work and at the weekends to sing in various places. After a few spots in the working men clubs I was getting theatre opportunities all over Northern Ireland and went as far as Ballyshannon with my singing friend Alison Hollywood who is now a successful singer/songwriter in London..

We always had some craic travelling everywhere in our car with my parents and it was like Alison was becoming my singing sister and in actual fact we sang the song 'Sisters, sisters, there never were the devoted sisters' with a routine that always went down a storm. We needed to take every opportunity to get on a stage and that's what we did.

Even though I wanted to perform in both acting and singing when you are that young, you just look at every avenue and take every opportunity. I looked up to any performer that was hugely successful so as a young hopeful when I met Ireland's First Lady of Country Susan McCann, I was looking up to her singing in front of all these people, making them happy and more importantly making my parents happy, so of course I wanted to sing those songs too and see the happiness on both their faces and make them proud.

I don't think I ever just wanted to be a singer you know standing up like Susan McCann, as me. I thought it was amazing but as time went on I started to get nervous standing up 'as Pauline' and singing. I think there was a real desire in me that I wanted to sing at the same time as playing different characters and I don't know if that was because I had things going on mentally. Was that the beginning of my mental health issues or was this just a natural progression, finding what made me tick. I just felt more comfortable being someone else.

So I began to act out what I saw the actors do on the T.V. and then do it my way. I would say to myself "if I was in love, this is how I would feel" little did I know that this was actually a technique that I would later learn at drama school by Konstantin Stanislavski, a Russian Theatre Practitioner and I was doing it instinctively.

I was always really dramatic and loved acting out lines from the movie Kramer Vs Kramer starring Dustin Hoffman and Meryl Streep.

"I love you God damn it"

When I got a scholarship to New York to train in acting when I was fifteen, I thought I was brilliant saying that live over and over in my perfectly practised American accent

"I love you God damn it, don't you understand how I feel about you?"

Until I was told that "damn it" was a swear word worse than fuck, I was mortified. After that I thought it was best to stick to my own language for a while.

That didn't stop me from doing well in New York though. I was picked up from the airport in a limo to be taken to a top Performing Arts School to train in acting, singing and dance. I was in heaven! I even did Off Broadway Showcases and performed in front of many Casting Directors and Agents who were really interested in me. One of them even contacted me and I found myself going Down Town New York to see a top New York Agent.

Agent – "Well Pauline, we are very interested in you. The only problem is we need you to get a green card so that you can work here. The easiest way to get that is if you have an American parent. So I am willing to adopt you. What do ya say kid?"

Pauline – "Oh my God. I'm the only person to come all the way to New York to be groomed by a paedophile. No thanks!

Besides I wanted to have my name Pauline Carville in lights not the name Nicole Star or some other name.

When I got home I was really excited about watching the T.V. thinking 'that could be me' and yet I was happy to be home and the more I thought about it … "Why would I want to live with some kiddie fiddler, when I have everything I want here?"

I did have some great experiences in New York though. I took lots of children to their auditions in New York cabbing it from one end of New York to another for movie and commercial auditions, some of whom went on to star in shows such as The Cosby Show, 90210 and A Different World. Getting a chance to live in that world was amazing however at this stage, although I would have loved working in New York later in my career, at fifteen, it just wasn't the right time.

I knew that if I wanted to be an actor and a singer I had to have a plan. I knew that I needed to have the right training in all three disciplines' acting, singing and dance. I had to make sure I was good at everything. To be honest, everything I put myself into, like sports, roller skating, even swimming I challenged myself to be good. I wanted to be good at everything. I competed with myself to always get better, to become the best at anything I did. Maybe that was the reason I became a perfectionist and my own worst critic.

Chapter 3 - Who Are The Carvilles?

My Daddy, Brendan, lived as a young boy in Templetown, a sleepy seaside neighbourhood, just outside Carlingford, County Louth. He was from a better off family than a lot of the kids down there as his Daddy had a job on the trains at the time. He had such a kind heart. He would walk down those wee track roads in his bare feet, just like the other kids who had no shoes. So he would leave his house with his shoes on and then would take them off at the bottom of the lane and put them into the hedges in front of his house for safekeeping. He was obviously quite a sensitive wee fella himself. He didn't want to be the odd one out. Do you know what I mean?

Then as a teenager his family moved to Belfast and he began working in the Belfast Brewery on the Glen Road. He did long distance lorry driving across the Irish Border to the (Free State) delivering soft drinks including Fanta and Coke a Cola and beers including the very popular Tennant's and Harp lagers.

He would tell us "If you knew how beer was made you wouldn't touch it" which is why he didn't. He never drank and when anyone tried to persuade him he would just repeat "I'm telling you, If you saw how it was made you wouldn't touch it". He also said "he would see rats swimming in it, so if that doesn't put you off I don't know what will"

Mind you, there used to be lots of alcohol in our house because he would get free beer and soft drinks as that was one of the perks of the job. It would pile up, so it was certainly great for our Deirdre and Geraldine's boyfriends when they were at drinking age, to have a fully stocked beer bar.

My Daddy had a pretty quiet existence. He worked his 6am to 2pm shift at the brewery one week and 2pm to 10pm the next week. He was mostly on the road and as he got older he was based more in the Brewery packing and other duties.

My Mummy Sheila was born in Aghagallan, just outside Moira, County Armagh. That's actually where she met my Daddy, just beside the railway track. She was twenty six and still living at home when she met him and he asked her out on a date. Weirdly enough when she met Daddy her family were moving to Belfast as their houses were being knocked down to make better roads into Belfast. She worked in the stitching factory, which were popular places of work at that time. They were moving into my Great Aunt Peg's house. She lived in Cavendish Street, just off the Falls Road, opposite the Royal Victoria Hospital.

Aunt Peg had lived there for years and I knew that she was to marry a US Naval officer, who she met whilst he was here on duty during the Second World War. He was then posted abroad. They would write the most romantic love letters to one another, until she received the devastating news that he had been killed in action.

She never really got over his death. Mummy always said that it completely changed her personality. She became very hard and you can imagine why, as she kept all that pain inside. Mummy said she was particularly strict with her when she was dating Daddy and tried to stop her from going out, saying that she had chores to do, yet Mummy was a grown woman. It was obviously difficult for her to see young love blossom again realising what she had lost. |

Aunt Peg was very good to us. She would walk all the way up the Falls Road to our house in Brooke Close. She regularly came to our house with sweets and treats. We were like her surrogate children I suppose. She was probably about sixty five at the time. It is weird how people of that generation looked older. They didn't dye their grey hair or try to keep themselves looking young as we do today. Aunt Peg had silver grey long hair that she held back in a low bun at the base of her head. I know in the end she couldn't walk and had to get the bus and my brothers and sisters and I would meet her coming up Brooke Drive. No wonder she had sore legs all that walking. She would wrap bandages around her feet and legs as she was still determined to walk, to see us.

I remember she started to get forgetful and stopped remembering our names. That's when she came to live in our house. Aunt Peg was diagnosed with breast cancer and went into hospital shortly after.

You see my Mummy was the most gentle, considerate, understanding and generous woman you could ever meet. She had so much love inside her and she looked after everyone. She even took care of a new neighbour who had moved into our street and didn't have any money for food and clothes for her three children, My Mummy would buy extra groceries and clothes for them for a very long time, she considered them like family and wanted to help.

Funny how people forget though because as soon as the neighbour got on her feet they moved out to an area they believed was more posh than where we lived and because she didn't want anyone to ever find out about her poor background she was never in contact with my Mummy again which really hurt her, as you can imagine..

I have two older sisters, Deirdre was the eldest, then Geraldine fourteen months younger, and an older brother Michael. I had another sister before me, she had Spina Bifida and a hole in her heart and sadly died at birth. I also have a younger brother Brendan.

Deirdre and Geraldine were like twins and they used to do everything together. I suppose you could say I was a bit jealous of them. They always had each other to talk to and they always seemed to be laughing, I didn't have that. They seemed much older than me at the time. Eight years then seemed like a huge gap and they appeared really old.

I would have had to listen to all their issues, all their boyfriend troubles, fights with their friends and needless to say fights with one another.

They both had part time jobs in Delaney's in Lombard Street, in the city centre and God love them, they only earned £6.00 for an eight to ten hour shift on a Saturday.

Delaney's was a café and served gorgeous homemade food and cakes. In fact their cakes were the talk of the town. Everyone went to Delaney's because they had the most amazing pavlova, lemon Meringue pie, apple tart and apple crumble and their portions were incredibly big. So you can imagine there was always a queue to get into Delaney's. When you did get in, you had to get in line to order your food, while someone went in search for a table, the best tables were up on the balcony style area. They had dark wood railings that separated the different parts and you knew which area you liked, it also had booths. It was ahead of its time. I think Delaney's is a place we will always remember. Funnily enough our Geraldine's husband also worked there as a chef. She didn't go out with him while they both worked there, that was later.

So Geraldine would save her money weekly to buy the best of gear while Deidre would go out and party. Deirdre would regularly borrow Geraldine's clothes behind her back and I use the word borrow lightly, as I am sure our Geraldine would put me straight and say "She stole my good clothes Pauline"

It wasn't the first time my daddy had to pull them both apart with Geraldine holding on to that coveted mint green trouser suit with both hands, while Deirdre had her hands wrapped tightly around Geraldine's long curly locks of hair. They would usually be on the floor at the same time screaming at each other and you could hear the frustration in Geraldine's voice

"Awk Daddy I saved for months for that suit and she was sneaking behind my back and going to wear it out"

If Deirdre had the trousers on Geraldine would be stripping them off her with brute force. Every time, they went for one another's hair and all you would hear over the house was

"Let go" said Deirdre

"No, you let go" Geraldine would say

"You let go first" Said Deirdre

"No, you let go first" Geraldine replied

And would you believe that they got on so well everyone would say "there's the Carville twins"

However those good old "Carville twins" would torture me. They would no doubt disagree with me now as they wouldn't have believed they were doing anything wrong, but my two sisters would keep me awake at night with the trials and tribulations of Deirdre's love life but I will keep that for later.

Deirdre said "I can't believe he said that to me, can you? I should have given him a good crack around the face like Sister Margarita use to tell us to do when a boy said something we didn't like"

"I know, Deirdre, you were a bit behind the door there. Do you remember when Mickey Devlin didn't see the slap coming and nearly fell into the DJ's Box? We nearly wet ourselves laughing. And what about the time your man Stevie Davidson ended up with a Babycham over his head for saying you had a nice bum? Said Geraldine

"Yes Geraldine, but I was only doing what the nuns said to do if a boy commented on your "bottom" but to tell you the truth I was delighted he liked my ass but I thought I couldn't let him know and thought I have to teach him a lesson and the Babycham was in my hand and without thinking too much about it, it was over his head. Mind you I was raging afterwards for wasting my drink."

Michael was my older brother by 3 years and Brendan was eighteen months younger than me. I don't remember a lot about our Michael when I was really young, however we became really close when I was a teenager and he became my best friend. I finally had someone that I could talk to about anything, things that I was worried about or if I went out with somebody he would give me advice.

Our Michael was my teenage confidante and I knew he would keep anything I told him to himself and vice versa. That is what I meant about being jealous of my sisters when I was younger because they had each other and I had no one as Michael was much older than me, until I was about fourteen and a bit more mature we had more in common then. I always looked up to our Michael and started to hang about with him and his friends and in actual fact I fancied one of them, Gregory….. I fancied the pants off him and did so since I was about eleven years old and that severe crush continued for years. Gregory was also a really good friend and did help me through some traumatic times and I suppose I could even say that when I went to Drama School in Glasgow Michael and Gregory visited me and I still held that crush a little even though deep down inside I knew at this time he definitely wasn't for me. If you ask me, Gregory was well and truly my first love, although I don't think he ever knew that.

I remember by the time I was twenty, Michael and I were as thick as thieves. I was totally gutted because he couldn't get a job here as unemployment was so bad and he and his friend had decided to move to London for a year. I was totally devastated and I would write to him every day, it is so weird to think of putting pen to paper to talk to your brother and best friend but we didn't have mobile phones and Mummy definitely wouldn't have let me phone him on the house phone as much as I would have wanted to, so I could get his advice on everything.

He came back after a year and it was probably a good thing because he had seen a different kind of life and what life was like in other places. He lived in Hastings which was a two hour journey up to London to work at the underground; he was there for his eight hour day and then a two hour journey back to Hastings. When he came back he then had the experience to get a job here so it was all worth it.

Our Brendan being the youngest was known in our house as "Mummy's Boy". He was only eighteen months younger than me but he always seemed much younger. Mummy always sat Brendan on one side of her and me on the other to read us stories when we were kids. I also recall our Brendan going to a weekly boxing class and regularly practising on me. It would really frustrate me as I had visions of my brother punching me in the face and you may have guessed, one day that actually happened. He was practising his boxing routine on me and this time he punched me right in the nose. I thought he had broken it. I was in such shock, I couldn't believe it. And believe me when I say that this was the last time he practised his boxing on me after I was finished with him.

Me with Deirdre, Michael and Geraldine

Deirdre, Geraldine, Michael, me and Brendan

Me and Michael

Me and Brendan

Mummy and daddy on their wedding day

Chapter 4 - Sunday Mornings In Our House

My daddy had a fun happy go lucky personality and although Mummy could be fun, she also had a more serious side. Well to be fair, she was the one who got us up in the mornings. Whilst Daddy was at work Mummy would be the disciplinarian. She could be stern at times and if we did something wrong you would be getting that glared look from Mummy, telling you that you were in trouble - not Daddy.

Mummy went through a stage of comparing us all to the neighbours in our street "Mary's children wouldn't behave like that" or "Eileen's daughter wouldn't speak to her the way you speak to me", you get the gist. So anyone knowing what it was like on a Sunday in our house would be a disaster in my Mummy's eyes. "What would the neighbours think?" So when our Geraldine won a prize for the best story in school my Mummy went mad.

Sunday mornings always started with Mummy trying to get us all out of bed and you'd think that my brother Brendan and I, the two youngest of 5 siblings, that we would be up playing games and causing havoc? Oh no … I was the second youngest and I would be shattered.

You see, I would have been put to bed early, at the same time as my younger brother, Brendan, which to me was so cruel. Mummy would say "You need your beauty sleep Pauline" I would get really annoyed and cry out "But our Brendan is younger than me and it's light outside". I could still hear my friends playing in the street, so I felt completely hard done by. Well why were they allowed out to that time and I wasn't. Didn't they need their shut eye? It was only 7.30pm and I was ten. And I bet you they wouldn't go through the torture that abated me every Saturday night, so you know wonder I didn't want to go to bed, let alone at that time.

You see, I didn't want to go to bed that early because at 1am Sunday morning, I would, like clockwork, be woken up by my two older sisters coming in from the Greenan Lodge, St. Paul's or the Kerry Inn, with a blow by blow account of their night.

The first thing I would hear would be the front door closing with the incessant silent giggling, then the creaking of the stairs as they crept slowly and sneakily up each stair, so as not to wake Mummy or Daddy. They didn't seem to have that consideration for me ... oh no, our Deirdre, the eldest of the two, would pull down on the door handle and fall in through the door with Geraldine, falling on top of her.

"Turn the light on" Deirdre would whisper "I can't see" say's Geraldine, the giggles would start. "Get off me, you silly bitch" from Deirdre. Then Geraldine would get up, trip over a pair of Deirdre's shoes and bang into the wall and as she pats around, looking for the light switch. The main light would go on, which, what seems like an. 100 watt bulb, so bright, instantly made me wide awake.

Then, there would be a detailed dissection of the happenings, the non- happenings, the likes, the dislikes, who got a good lumber (Belfast saying for a kiss...without tongues) and by God if Deirdre didn't get one, she would nag on about it, all night and so, no chance of me getting to sleep. (By the way, Deirdre still loves to lumber today!)

That wouldn't be the end of it though. Deirdre had to make

sure her hair was ready for Sunday mass, so she would continue to rabbit on about her latest non conquest whilst pin curling her hair. This was like a military operation and by God, you didn't want her to have had Gin - why? Well, I know they say 'gin makes you sin' but gin makes our Deirdre cry and a frustrated me had to watch her organising the pin curls, crying about the lack of lumber and her anger towards the pin curls.

"These fuckin pin curls won't go in and I need them for Mass in the morning or my hair will be a mess" A calm Geraldine would respond

"You know what Deirdre, he doesn't deserve you. You know he's the type to try it on and you'd have to give him a good slap anyway"

(That's the advice from the Nuns in our school once again).

Sister Margarita in a Southern Irish accent "If his hands wander, give him a good slap"

I said in my strong West Belfast accent "Well I wonder, would you both shut the fuck up? … That's my advice"

So needless to say, I couldn't get up on Sunday morning's when Mummy starts to gulder (West Belfast for shout) upstairs "get up" in her foghorn voice.

This was not a good start for mummy's Sunday morning form. She'd already lost her grey shoes and matching handbag, as she did every Sunday. If it wasn't the grey, it was the black or the red. Mummy always had matching shoes and bags.

Breakfast was noisy enough in our house with my parents and two brothers and two sisters. We were all trying to compete for the attention, but when Geraldine remembered her good news about her essay "Sunday mornings in our house" for her English O' Level, well that was an explosion worse than the bomb at the Greenan Lodge the week before.

Mummy at the start was really excited that Geraldine had done really well and was going to get a prize at her Prize day she said "Well go and get it and read it to us".

She was soon sorry, she said that, because the very talented Geraldine had written the funniest account of mummy losing her shoes on a weekly basis, burning the breakfast and blaming all of us for not getting out of bed when she called and then being late for Mass (which was a cardinal sin) round our way.

"I can't believe you told your teacher all that. "What will she think? What will everyone think when they hear about this? Mummy screamed.

It went from that to mummy being on her hands and knees crawling, looking for her shoes behind the sofa where she would throw them when the milkman would arrive to get paid, to keep the place tidy she would say.

She was so distraught and angry and Godlove her, hilariously repeating what Geraldine wrote in the story, that Daddy would step in, silently guiding us out to the back garden, leaving Mummy in the house screaming at the walls while we were outside wetting ourselves laughing. Our house on Sunday morning was mayhem and a pure geg. (West Belfast for a laugh).

CHAPTER 5 - CAUGHT ON RIGHTLY

Mummy would have been the parent, I would be afraid of, if I did something wrong for example, the summer afternoon Mr Goldsmith in Brooke Crescent caught me smoking when I was thirteen.

Mr Goldsmith in his 'I caught you' tone "Now I am sure if your mummy saw you smoking she would not be too happy with you. Would she?

Pauline - "No Mr Goldsmith" shaking with fear, my voice was an octave higher than usual.

Mr Goldsmith - "So what do you think you should do?"

Pauline - "Put it out Mr Goldsmith?"

Mr Goldsmith - "Yes, but you should also go and tell your mummy that you were smoking so that I don't have to"

Pauline - "Yes Mr Goldsmith"

Well, that's how good a child I was. Sure didn't I go straight home to tell my mummy that Mr Goldsmith had caught me smoking? Was I mad or what? Well I thought she's going to kill me!

Imagine getting caught by him, of all people, sure wouldn't the whole neighbourhood find out about it? Well, that's why I didn't take any chances of my mummy finding out from someone else. That's why I decided on the spot to go and tell her … she would find out anyway … she always did.

When I got to the house mummy was having a nap on the sofa. I think at this time she had started going through the menopause because before this mummy was really great fun, like she would dress up at Halloween and go round the doors singing "Halloween coming on a and the goose is getting fat" but not this year.

Every afternoon mummy would grab her wee blue and white checked blanket that she would often throw around her shoulders in the kitchen when it was nippy, making herself a wee cup of Riddle Marie (Belfast for cup of tea) and sing once again "Good Look'n Woman and other Joe Dolan hits.

Recently, afternoons were for the forty winks that was required for a "wee rest of the eyes" for 10 minutes, 30 minutes or an hour depending on how much her eyes needed a rest, if you get my meaning. The menopause was pretty hard on my mummy.

Of course this was the worst time for me to bear my soul. Mummy never woke up out of those forty winks in good form, so what made me think she would want to wake up to this?

Me, this innocent thirteen year old, just needed to get it off my chest…. I know you don't get many innocent thirteen year olds these days, they could buy and sell you today and that's saying something, but I think my generation mostly were innocent at that age and I certainly was.

Pauline - "Mummy?" That quiet call, nearly not making a sound at all … no response

Pauline - "Mummy?" A bit louder …

Pauline - "Mummy? I need to tell you something!

Well, I was trying to gently ease her out of her sleep

"What?" Mummy said. It wasn't even really loud but I could hear the annoyance in her voice. She clearly wasn't ready to be awake.

Well the sound of her voice made me jump out of my skin, this was a very tricky situation, so I ran crying up the stairs passing Daddy in the hallway as he arrived home from work. I was crying my eyes out, you would have thought I had killed someone.

Daddy followed me upstairs to see what was wrong. Daddy always had this calmness about him and that made it easy for me to confess this dreadful sin of smoking and being caught "into the bargain" (West Belfast "as if it wasn't bad enough).

Daddy "What's wrong love" in his chocolate toned soothing voice

Choking back the tears and gasping to get my breath back. Didn't I start to feel guilty now, because not only did Mr Goldsmith catch me smoking, Daddy was going to ask where I got the fegs from (West Belfast for cigarettes) and now the guilt was over riding the actual "caught on smoking" event.

I just spat it out.

Pauline - "You know the gap between the two houses, just at the entrance of Brooke Crescent, hidden behind the trees? Well me and Linda were smoking and Mr Goldsmith caught us, and he said he was going to tell mummy, so I wanted to tell her myself, and I'm really sorry daddy – I stole two cigarettes from your twenty deck of Benson & Hedges on the china cabinet, one for me and one for Linda".

As I sobbed away daddy put his arm around me and said

"Well, did you enjoy it??"

"What" I said, completely confused. "Being caught?"

Daddy "No, the cigarette?"

"No daddy" I said "It wasn't worth it"

Daddy in his understanding voice said

"If you decide you want to try smoking again, sure let me know, ask me and I will give you the full pack of twenty and you can smoke every last one ... that will put you off smoking for life"

I just looked at him totally confused now. No anger, no disappointed looks. He was going to give me all twenty fegs to smoke?

He then said:

"I started smoking when I was eight in the bathroom at our house. I would put the shower on and hung out the window puffing away like a good'n. I just wished someone had have caught me back then, I certainly wouldn't be addicted now"

Of course I was still panting breathlessly from the crying. I had just admitted something that could potentially get me into trouble and daddy just finished by saying

"So calm yourself down and dry those tears, it's not the end of the world"

I was so relieved and should have known that that wouldn't be the end of it.

Didn't daddy go downstairs and Mummy had asked him what was wrong with me, not a big deal to him, he explained what had happened.. Well that was it, Mummy jumped off the sofa, as quickly as she had got on it 30 minutes before.

There was a silence of what seemed like three seconds, whilst Mummy got to the bottom of the stairs and then all I heard was the stomp, stomp, and stomp on the stairs. Didn't I tell you Mummy was the disciplinarian? She, in no uncertain terms, told me that I wasn't allowed out of our street for two whole weeks and I was no longer allowed to go about with Linda ever again. Well that was going to be a disaster as Linda's parents went away regularly and as she was older than me she would have great house parties, what was I going to do now?

Daddy didn't tell her that I provided the stolen cigarettes, not Linda.

A few weeks later when Mr Goldsmith saw me again he winked at me and said

"Your secret is safe with me!"

I couldn't believe this. I had just done time, for two whole weeks because of that clampet! Or was I the clampet?? (West Belfast for Dick Head).

Chapter 6 - Christmas Memories

I always looked forward to Christmas in our house, the excitement of Santa arriving. I loved winter and the feeling in the air, the bright lights, the atmosphere. I still do actually, you know, sitting at the edge of your seat wondering what you were going to get for Christmas?

I remember my best present, which is now completely illegal and certainly not politically correct and even racist was Gollywog dolls and teddy bears. They were a really popular thing when I was younger and my favourite present was the year I got my two biggest presents together. A giant teddy bear gollywog, it was bigger than me and I was about eight and my roller boots, God the things I would do on those roller boots, me and Janine would make up dance routines and thought that we were so good that we could be on 'Starlight Express'.

This particular Christmas I was just so excited, I loved that gollywog like other children would love a dog for Christmas. I couldn't believe Santa had brought me my dream present. I remember Mummy and Daddy coming down the stairs and how much I loved them. I knew that they had arranged Santa to give me what I really wanted. I could see on their faces how happy they were. I was so happy and I was hugging that gollywog with my entire mite.

I remember the song "Words" by F. R. David was playing on the record player; someone had got the album 'That's what I call Music'. I was so ecstatic in that moment as the song to me was so apt because I was so happy and didn't have the words to express how I felt. All I could do was hug the gollywog and then throw my arms around Mummy and Daddy in thanks, I still couldn't find the words to say thank you, the hug, I believed said it for me. This was probably the happiest I had ever been, as I can remember anyway.

So between the gollywog and then roller boots, the gollywog was my way of being able to express my love and the roller boots was a way for me to express my creative self. I didn't know what to do because I wanted to spend time with my golly, but I also wanted to use my roller boots, so I was completely torn. Of course roller boots were an upgrade from our old metal skates with red leather straps. Roller boots had a smoother ride and also had stoppers at the front making it easier to manoeuvre.

Janine had also got roller boots and she had called up to my house and said

"Are you coming out?"

I said "But I have so many things I want to play with"

"Ah come on Pauline, let's do some new routines and we can practice doing jumps and lifts and everything"

Of course when Janine and I were doing any lifts we would both take turns on who was actually being lifted up. This particular day we were dancing to "It's gonna be a long night" from the T.V. series 'Fame' and we were so good at that, every move we did, worked really well and so we decided it was time to challenge ourselves on the lifts and we both looked at each other and said

"'Flashdance' "What a feeling".

I was wearing my Christmas clothes so was Janine and mine was a little maroon jersey style dress and I felt lovely in it and Janine was wearing a little winter white polo neck jumper with a red, short, ballet style wrap skirt with tights and we were both wee skinny things and we thought we looked like perfect roller boot dancers.

Janine said very determinedly "It's my turn, it's my turn to do the lift, so you will have to lift me"

I was saying "AK no! Please, Janine let me do it, I love 'FlashDance' you know it's my favourite song"

Janine said "No Pauline, you promised the last time"

Oh well a promise is a promise, so we started practising.

"First when there's nothing,

But, a slow flowing dream,

That your fear seems to hide, deep inside your mind"

We were doing all these great moves and lovely turns and up and down arm movements

"All alone I have cried,

Silent tears, full of pride,

In a world made of steel,

Made of stars"

The plan was that Janine was going up on to my shoulders at

"Made of ….. And rested on the shoulders at "Stars" so that we would start moving forward on "What a feeling" turn on "Seeing's believing" and coming back. That was the plan.

However when Janine got onto my shoulders at "stars" I felt a very hot feeling on my shoulders and I said

"Janine, there's something wrong, there's something wrong with my shoulders"

Then it started to dribble down my arms and back and onto my hands and I thought

"What the fuck is this?" and when I smelt my hand I realised and screamed

"You've fuckin pissed yourself"

 I dropped her to the ground. She had fuckin pissed on me with the excitement of getting up on to my shoulders. She was so excited that she had got that bit right. Obviously we didn't get the chance to be successful on the next bit and "What a Feeling" because the piss was pissing down my body and I thought its Christmas Fuckin Day and I am going to get killed, thankfully, I had already been to Mass, so that wasn't an issue, but I knew my mummy was going to go mad.

So that was the end of my dance partnership with Janine. We never danced again.

So that memory was the Christmas that I got everything I wanted and I could see how happy mummy and daddy were and everyone got everything they wanted.

There was, however, one Christmas, when my Daddy hadn't been well and in truth it had been a really bad year for them as Mummy hadn't been well that year either. My Daddy had been off work with a bad back for three months running up to this Christmas and he was the breadwinner in our house.

As I mentioned before Deirdre and Geraldine worked in Delaney's and they used to spend their money on whatever they wanted, usually clothes and shoes and going out. This year they knew they needed to save their pay up to help my parents pay for Christmas. My younger brother Brendan still believed in Santa and it may have been his last year believing, so they still wanted to make it special.

That particular year there were the wee warnings

"You know, Santa may not be able to give you everything that you want this year. Santa is very busy and there are lots of children needing presents."

For about twelve Saturday's, I knew my sisters were saving their money to help out, I knew what was going on, sure I would always hear them talking and this time was no different. I no longer believed in Santa. I would hear Deirdre say to Geraldine

"Have you saved all your money?"

"Yes" Geraldine replied

"What are we going to do about our Christmas clothes for Mass on Christmas Day?" said Deirdre "Has mummy got Christmas clothes for Michael, Pauline and Brendan?"

I could see Daddy wasn't well and with all the conversations I was witnessing and Deirdre and Geraldine were always buying the best of gear, I was wondering if they would have enough money to purchase their own Christmas clothes. I mean our Deirdre would have had those black shiny spandex all in one bodysuits with the shoes that Olivia Newton John wore in 'Grease' the actual shoes, so you can imagine they both normally went to town on picking their clothes. This Christmas was different! They hadn't bought anything for themselves.

Two Saturday's before Christmas they both handed Mummy an envelope and said

"That is everything we have saved"

I remember Mummy crying!

The strangest thing about all this was, on Christmas Day, I can't actually remember exactly what I got, but I do remember thinking, how could I have gotten what I wanted when they had struggled so much. It did certainly make me appreciate everything that Christmas, even the wee stocking fillers. I know Mummy was so stressed; she had hidden some of my presents and couldn't find them on time, to display on Christmas Eve. It was funny though, she was finding jewellery for me, for weeks after. I remember thinking

"Oh my God, not only has Mummy paid for this Christmas, so have my sisters"

That is what a West Belfast family is all about. They pull together!

It's funny because on Christmas, even my sisters came in and mummy said

"Did you get what you needed?"

They then showed her what they had got. They had timed every week perfectly so that on that last Saturday that they worked before Christmas, they were able to get their clothes for Christmas Day.

Of course, Daddy didn't know all this was going on. Mummy kept telling him not to worry and that everything was sorted.

When I think about it, all Deirdre and Geraldine received in their pay on a Saturday; this certainly puts things into perspective for what we spend today. That was probably the hardest Christmas I remember and seeing how everyone had pulled together, it was also one of the best Christmas's we ever had.

CHAPTER 7 - BELGIUM: THE NIGHTMARES ARE BACK!

In East and West Belfast in the 80's, there was a project set up (Project Children) I think it was called, for the young teens to get a chance to go and stay, kind of like a respite from the troubles in Belfast and they were placed with a family in America or Europe. I wanted to be an actor, so I thought "Oh I will definitely get to America, this will be my opportunity". You see, when I was younger I wanted to be 'American'; in fact, I couldn't believe that I wasn't. I couldn't accept that my mummy and daddy had to come from Northern Ireland, I mean trust my luck. Of course I think very differently now, but back then I thought, "Oh happy days I am going to get to America"

Unfortunately America was not on the cards for me, not at this point anyway. Instead, I ended up in Belgium.

ZONHOVEN

In fact not only did I end up in Belgium, I ended up in a house, on a motorway with the very sign ZONHOVEN outside my bedroom window. It is funny when I think of it, especially when we were driving down the motorway, I would see so many different styles and sizes of houses and my imagination was running away with me. So when the bus began to slow down there was a big white house coming up on my right and I thought, wouldn't it be amazing if I was staying there? So when they stopped outside the red brick sixties looking box and called out my name I was totally gutted. But me, being me, I put a big smile on my face and pretended everything was going to be alright.

On the plane, travelling to Belgium, I was very positive, I was eleven, my mummy and daddy didn't really want me to go, but I was pretty street wise as a child, I was from the West, so you know? I was very independent and I wanted to have this experience and mummy kept saying

"Pauline you are too young to be going away on your own "and I would say

"That's the whole point, young enough to experience new things, away from here. I am going to stay with a family, they will look after me, so don't be worrying."

So the school reassured her and mummy and daddy agreed.

So all the Project Children were going on the same flight and everybody was going to different places, Belgium, Germany, Luxemburg and as I said I was going to Belgium.

I remember the Nuns from our school were also on the flight, because of course our school did have many nuns as teachers. The nuns always had southern Irish accents and they would say;

"Oh you are going to have a wonderful time, you will be doing so many exciting things and you will meet a lovely family to stay with.". It was fun on the plane and all the other kids, some of my school friends were excited too.

However, as soon as I met the family ….. To say they looked strange was an understatement.

They were weird and they had faces on them like Lurgan

Spades. (West Belfast for miserable faces)

Boy, were they happy to see me? …. Not!

Yeah they didn't look too pleased to be having me and of course they would have gone through a procedure and chosen to do all this. So to be honest I had this really, really bad feeling, a sixth sense you could call it. They thought they were getting a little Irish Leprechaun from West Belfast and instead ….. Got me!

Truthfully when I look back I think to myself

"Oh my God when I turned up, I was no leprechaun, I was a tall, lanky, short haired, you could say, ugly mug, because I had really thin hair and mummy had this hairdresser Liz and she always recommended that the best thing for thin hair at my age, was to keep trimming it …. So that is exactly what my mummy did. So I looked like …. A boy and wait for it … in a navy and white flowery dress. Now I was eleven, my mummy thought I was still …. Five and she was trying to clearly keep her youngest daughter, young, for as long as she could. Needless to say they didn't look pleased when they saw me.

Truthfully my hair looked like Liz the hairdresser had cut my hair with a bowl around it or not too far away from that. It was a boy's haircut. I know she did ladies haircuts and I don't want to offend anyone, but my mummy made me go to this hairdresser right up to the age of fourteen when I was trying to grow my fringe out for our Deirdre's wedding (I will explain later)

So, the Belgians didn't look too pleased to see me. They must have thought "What have we let ourselves in for". Me? I just had uneasiness in the pit of my stomach, something bad was going to happen.

I was from a noisy, lively, family ….. They were so not lively and not even a bit noisy, they were dour. How can I explain …? Hard faced …. And they didn't look very happy ….. So I felt very uncomfortable. I did try to be open minded and friendly, as you would, chatting away in my friendly, dark toned, West Belfast accent.

"Hello, my name is Pauline"

They just glared at me! I thought, are they glaring at me because they don't understand what I am saying nor do they not speak English? I mean why would you have an eleven year old girl or any child for that matter if you don't speak English? When I went into the house, I had an unusually cold feeling that came over me. Strange! I did have my own bedroom though.

I kept staring at this 13 year old that I was staying with. Her name was Hannah. God, if I thought I was pretty ugly at that time, Oh my Lord she was a redhead but a funny looking red, an ugly red and she had these glasses on that made her eyes look like they were popping out of her head. Now I do have to say she did have very nice lips. They were the kind of lips you would definitely like now. I kept looking at them because they were very pouty before pouty became a thing.

She was very well endowed for her years; she was thirteen, very tall, taller than me and something very masculine about her. Even though I too looked like a boy because of the way mummy had my hair, how I looked, it did not match who I was. I was a feminine wee thing at that time trying to get out and dying to let my girly side out …. My mummy obviously had other ideas.

She was obviously confused with the dress in one respect and the hair, on the other. God love my mummy she was trying to do her best for me so that I could have the long locks I have today. As they say "beauty is pain" and boy did I suffer at the hands of my mummy and Liz the old ladies hairdresser.

From the first day in Belgium, I had the worst nightmares. I also remembered having severe nightmares when I was around eight years old. I couldn't remember why I had been having the bad dreams back then; all I knew was that they were back! I went from this happy go lucky child to this stressed, well I don't know if I knew what stress was, so I suppose it was just a fear within me.

One, I thought I was never going to see my mummy and daddy again.

Two, I thought that something was going to happen to me and they would never know where I was or what happened to me.

Three, I was just petrified!

I didn't really understand where the fear was coming from and as the first days passed, the family really weren't that bad. They were really pleasant. They were just struggling with the language, trying so hard to make me feel at home. But I guess they weren't expecting to have a wee girl staying with them that was crying through the night in her nightmares and then crying morning, noon and night.

I really was scared and yet when my mummy rang I played the role of "I am happy as Larry mummy, I am fine" I was dying to tell her that I hated it but I knew her and my daddy didn't have the money to get me home. So I sucked it up and got on with it, which would be my downfall later. Sad really when you think about it. I was just terrified and actually when I put myself into that memory, in that situation I get that feeling like it was yesterday. It was the most frightening thing that I had ever been in my entire life.

I kept dreaming that maybe I would be lucky to get to go into that big house. The sun shone on it every day like it was the place to be. It was so majestic and I felt so frustrated that I wasn't staying with that family. Oh how things could have been different.

So I wasn't enamoured by the family I was staying with. I did meet the girl who lived in the big house across the road just after a few days. Her name was Elena. She was ten, a year younger than me and a much younger version, if you know what I mean? She was definitely less streetwise than I was and I could tell, because, let's face it, I was from an estate, in the heart of the West, in an end terrace house, and she lived in the big white mansion on the hill.

She lived a very privileged life. To get to her house you had to drive up this sweeping driveway, uphill, a way up hill and oh, my, it was a mansion, I mean it was absolutely massive, in fact I don't think I had ever seen a house like it in my life, in person anyway. When I walked into that house, Oh my God, it was huge. It had white marble tiles and a big massive sweeping staircase it was like …. It was bigger than the Carrington house in the tv show Dynasty!

Elena had a brother. He was seventeen. I had never seen a boy with a moustache before and he had one. I never really thought much of him, he was much older than us and they were all really lovely people. There was a different feeling in that house, I felt safe. Elena's brother didn't appear to speak much English either. Her mummy and daddy were pretty fluent.

I was much happier with Elena; she was such a beautiful wee girl with a good heart. The difference between her and Hannah was like chalk and cheese.

So on this side of the road I was in this house on a motorway with the cars flying past, it felt like the house was actually part of the road by this Zonhoven sign. Elena's house was just like being in a completely different world.

Elena was so sweet and I took her under my wing and I was delighted, I now had a ally, she was now my friend and because I have always had a good sense of what people are like on first meeting, I knew she was going to be fun to be around and now I did feel a little more settled.

Although I was miserable and having nightmares, I still tried to have fun and with wanting to be an actress, I started to show Hannah some of the performances my friends and I would do at home. I would direct her in different songs and the popular commercials had great songs. This time it was the theme music of Pepsi Cola 'First Time' by Robin Beck. We would use old scarves in our hairs and ruffle up our skirts, so that we felt different. I was always trying to take my mind off the sleepless nights, the nightmares and what I began calling 'The Fears'. Performing was my solace and helped me to focus my mind on something else, so playing different characters and singing and dancing and showing Hannah and Elena the type of things I would be doing at home, taking the focus from my thoughts and the fact that I had pins and needles down my arms and hands with nerves and fear helped me through.

Hannah kept saying that we were going to a big park on Saturday that had a fun fair with fun rides like Blackpool, an animal park, big lakes and a place to have a picnic and ride bikes, which was a very popular activity in Belgium. Everyone seemed to be riding a bike wherever they went.

I thought the whole family was going and they brought Elena as well, so I was so delighted that she was coming too. Hannah's parents dropped us off to have our picnic alone and then we were going to be meeting them later for us all to go to the fun park to go on the rides, in the meantime they were going to entertain Hannah's brother.

So we walked around trying to find our perfect spot and as we thought we were big girls being alone with our picnic, which included sandwiches, crisps and a drink each. We decided on the end of a path that had a lake on each side of us and it was so lovely and I think for the first time I had started to relax a bit more with Hannah, I suppose because Elena was there too and liked her, she helped.

We were sitting giggling and laughing and I had probably been in Belgium about two weeks and trying my best to get the time through as quickly as possible. Hannah just wasn't very exciting but luckily I had Elena. She was good craic and it did help that she was a bit younger than me so I could look after her. I don't think Hannah liked it too much that we got on so well, but what could I do? Hannah always appeared to be in a mood!

So everywhere I looked everybody was on a bike cycling around the place, young and old and this fascinated me. We were laughing our heads off, when I noticed a man cycling towards us and he was saying something in the native language Flemish. I assumed it was "hello". He seemed pleasant and he kept speaking to the girls and they were politely responding. When I asked what he had said they told me he was asking if we were having a lovely day and enjoying the weather and where our parents were?

We didn't think anything of it at this time until he came around again and asked the same questions. Of course I didn't speak the language so I was looking at his facial expressions and listening to the tone of his voice and it appeared different. I got that really sick feeling in my stomach again, only this time it was stronger. I suggested to Hannah that we should go and get her parents and bearing in mind I mentioned earlier, my gut was saying that there might be something wrong. Hannah said that it was ok and that we should stay a little longer. The question "Where are your parents?" said it all to me.

I was a little worried when the man cycled past as once again. This time I got that sinking feeling that something bad was going to happen and now when he spoke I saw a shift in Hannah's reaction. I asked her, "What did he just say?" She said "Nothing, nothing", but I knew she was hiding something and I looked at Elena, she was oblivious. We carried on again, playing and acting out little shows as we always did and then here he was again.

This is when I really did get a negative feeling, I thought "there's something wrong here" and this time I saw Hannah's body language change and whatever that man was saying to her, I saw her face had changed.

My body instantly froze so I stood up; my survival instinct was setting in. I was getting ready to run if I had to. I knew something was wrong and of course I had had this feeling since I had arrived on Belgium soil.

As soon as I stood up, bearing in mind I am only eleven years old, but an eleven year old from Belfast, he jumped off his bike. I grabbed Elena to protect her, I didn't know what was going to happen but something was about to take place.

The man grabbed Hannah and from this moment on everything went into slow motion. That is what happens when something frightening happens, it goes into slow motion and you don't know what to do, whether to run or try and fight him off.

What was going through my mind was his bike was in the way of where I wanted to run. If I went to my right, there was a lake, so I would end up swimming in the frigging lake. So I was afraid that he could get me and at the same time I felt responsible for Elena.

I was so scared when I saw the man pulling Hannah to the ground and he was getting on top of her as he unzipped his trousers. When I tried to move he was able to grab me at the same time and what felt like a lifetime I fought him off, grabbed Elena and started to run at the same time I was shouting back to Hannah "I am going to get help, I am getting help"

As we ran I felt like my body wasn't taking me anywhere, it felt like I was in a horrible movie and I was freaking out about what was happening to Hannah whilst we were running. I was also feeling guilty for leaving her especially as we hadn't come across anyone yet.

Elena and I were both crying and screaming and were obviously in a terrible state, when we finally found this wee old man and woman. I felt like we were running forever and it felt like we were miles away from where Hannah was being attacked, but as it happened, afterwards the couple explained afterwards that we hadn't run that far, but it certainly felt far.

When we got back the man was still on top of Hannah and she was screaming for help! When he saw us he jumped up onto his bike and because the wee couple weren't very strong on their feet, they were unable to chase him. They did look after us whilst they called the Police.

My gut was right, something bad was going to happen and it just did. Hannah had been raped. My instinct to get her parents was also right. This was the beginning of my sixth sense. After this, I had severe anxiety that I kept hidden from everyone, including myself.

So we didn't get onto the rides or the roller coaster that they kept talking about. Oh no the only fucking roller coaster I was going to, was roller coasting into the police station and explaining everything that happened and their English was so bad you can imagine when we got back to the house, I felt like I had been through the mill. If my nightmares were bad before, this as you can imagine increased the terror, playing over and over in my head, what could have happened.

The next few days Hannah stayed in her room and didn't speak to anyone. She was totally traumatised. The man didn't get close to me or Elena however, we were affected too. We were able to talk to one another. Hannah wasn't the most talkative person to begin with, now she was silent and stared into space.

Elena's family offered to take me to their house to give Hannah and her parent's time to deal with their ordeal. We had a lovely dinner and then we played games. It was a great night and when it was time for bed, I was shown to my room.

I think Elena was in a different wing because the house was so big. I went to bed and here I was in another strange house and felt quite relaxed, until the moment that moustache boy walked into the room. I think he was around seventeen, but he was about six feet tall with dark hair, but to me he looked thirty five. He came and said in his foreign accent

"OK? OK?

I said "Yes ok"

"Bed good?

And I said "Yes the bed is comfortable"

I assumed that's what he meant, but what he was really asking was, if the bed was good enough for him to get in.

I went "What, what?" He started to walk towards me and he began lifting the covers

I said" what the fuck are you doing?"

He said "Getting in, getting in, you said bed is good"

And I said "Get away da fuck! Get out!"

I got up and pushed him out the door.

He then said "Just checking to see if bed was warm"

As much as I had the guts to tell him to fuck off, Hannah had just been assaulted the day before and I am now in the place where I thought I was safe with my wee mate and she is down on the other wing. Now her brother was trying to get into me, so twice on this trip my virginity was in danger of being lost and I didn't even know what that meant then. He was trying to get into bed with me, so what was his plan? Well I wasn't waiting around to find out.

I cried myself to sleep that night and I didn't want Elena's parents to have to deal with this and I didn't want to get Elena into trouble. So you could say I was protecting her and I know she looked up to me, especially after what had happened the day before. She thought I had saved her. I suppose I did, in a way.

The next day back over in the motorway Zonhoven house, I was turning over everything that had happened during and after the attack and the potential molestation of me by moustache boy I still pretended to mummy and daddy on the phone that everything was fine, because I knew they couldn't afford to get me home and I didn't want them to worry.

The nightmares had changed from the fear of getting home to my family to the ordeal for Hannah. I replayed what had happened in my head over and over and all I could see was that man unzipping his trousers and them dropping to the ground as he held her down with both hands as he climbed on top of her. I wasn't there to see what had really happened. My mind kept playing what I believed had happened and now I was disturbed and in complete shock.

When I finally got home, I was so relieved. I had never been so scared in my life.

As if that wasn't bad enough I was only back from Belgium for a week and I received a letter to say, the day after I left Elena was killed on the motorway as she was crossing to see Hannah. I was so devastated

After that I must have blocked it out…...

Chapter 8 - The First Family Wedding

My two sisters started dating two best friends. Well it wasn't really as simple as that. Our Deirdre was going to a school formal with a guy who had asked her to accompany him. They were driven by two friends who would become husbands to be for both Deirdre and Geraldine in the future.

She wore this all in one two tone silvery gold trouser suit which was highly fashionable in the 80's; in fact it would be gorgeous now if I was nice and skinny. She looked gorgeous, in fact our Deirdre and Geraldine always looked fabulous. They both had this beautiful long curly hair that I always envied; my hair was poker straight.

Whilst Deirdre, her date, and the two friends drove to the formal they stopped at the shop and so Deirdre had the chance to chat to one of them and I think in that moment Deirdre had thought "If I was gonna lumber anybody, it would be him". But unfortunately she was with "what's his name" and so she had to be good.

After the formal of course I would hear the full account of the night.

"He said this; he said that, I was so bored. If I didn't keep talking to him, there would have been pure silence, nothing. I just wished the other guy 'Sexy Boy' had been there" she meant of course, at the dancel.

Geraldine would say in response

"Well see at the end of the day, Deirdre, you know if you're man is interested, he'll ring ya"

Well the funny thing is that is exactly what happened. 'Sexy Boy' had asked 'boring guy' for Deirdre's number because she had left a little sparkly pashmina for her shoulders (very posh) in the car. I think she left it in the car on purpose to get that call!

After which 'Sexy Boy' asks Deirdre out on a date and once again, I get this blow by blow account of the date and how everything went, what he said, what she said and come to think of it, I am still getting blow by blow accounts of everything in her life forty years later. Well, that's what sisters do isn't it?

I was rather excited to meet this new man, because our Deirdre had gone on so much about him and how he had swept her off her feet and how he was absolutely gorgeous with jet black hair and I thought Adonis was going to walk in. Instead this West Belfast, duffle coated, long haired jetty proceeded through our door. Well that is what I called him at the time. I think I meant long haired yeti.

At first I was so disappointed because I thought, oh, she must be going for the personality. It was more because I hated men with long hair, long hair I thought, why would a man want long hair? But of course it was very popular at the time along with flares, long collared shirts and of course the duffle coat. The duffle coat by the way was also very fashionable at the time, especially up there in West Belfast. Mind you, it would have been better if it had been a dark navy, but his was brown.

Of course then I kept on hearing our Deirdre saying to our Geraldine

"You should go out with 'Sexy Boys friend'"

Not long after Geraldine began dating the friend and clearly into him. Well the two duffle coat yetti's and Deirdre and Geraldine were all going out and were both so happy. It was great to see and maybe the regular blow by blow accounts that I had been subjected to might finally end. Or was this just the beginning?   The next thing is, Deirdre announces that she is getting married. 'Sexy Boy' proposed!

God love Mummy and Daddy, the stress that they were under because Daddy didn't make a lot of money and in those days, the daughters parents paid for the wedding, although Deirdre and 'Sexy Boy' l had both said, "No, no, we are paying for our own wedding"

So it was getting to that stage where the Bride and Groom were becoming more independent so that they were in control of their wedding a bit more like what it is like today, mind you. I kept hoping that someone may want to pay for my wedding when it comes.

Of course my parents still wanted to help them. So the savings began, along with the house being taken apart. A full redecoration, after all, there were going to be a lot of visitors including the Groom's parents meeting the parents of the Bride and the house would have to look its best.

Then the arguments began, who was going to the wedding, who mummy wanted to go to the wedding, who Deirdre didn't want to go to the wedding and don't even start with me that didn't include his side of the family. You know the usual family feud about who can sit beside who, and who can't?

As you can imagine, the lead up to the wedding was tense.

Dress fittings and organising all our hairs to be styled. Speaking of hair! I was always trying to let my hair grow and Mummy had been constantly getting my haircut to thicken it up. I had spent the whole year growing it out and then Mummy announced that it was time to go back to the dreaded hairdresser.

"But mummy, I have been letting my hair grow, I have been growing out my fringe and I want it to grow to all the one length."

At this stage my hair was sitting just past my shoulders and my fringe was probably down at my cheek bone, but I would love a perm because perms were really in and as I mentioned before I always loved the idea of having curly hair like my sisters.

I said "I want a perm, you know that corkscrew look"

Mummy said "Sure Liz will do it for you"

I certainly didn't want to go back to her, but it was either that, or I didn't get my perm. Mind you I would have been better off not going at all and doing without the perm because of course what happened was Liz Scissorhands went against everything I said and chopped a fuckin fringe into my hair. I was absolutely gutted! As for the Perm? I looked like a fuzz buzz. It turned out worse than the one your woman Deirdre Barlow from Coronation Street got. Clearly Liz was absent the day they did perms in her hairdressing training.

You know what I looked like; I looked more like a fucking poodle and as for the wedding? I looked like a 'poodle's bridesmaid'!

The day of the wedding came and I was so excited because I fancied one of Deirdre's friends. You know when you are younger, you actually think you are much older than you are and think you are really mature and all, and I was thinking …. Today is my big chance to go out with what what I termed 'Sex on legs'. Oh God, he was sexy and he even had a moustache and normally I wouldn't usually be into boys with facial hair, but he really was sex on legs to me and every time he came to the table to arrange a round of drinks I'd say

"Yes, I'll have…. And I wanted to say something like "Vodka & Coke" but of course I'd have to say

"Lemonade"

I would be fluttering my eyes at him and I would be tossing my poodle perm back over my shoulders to sort of say, "fancy me baby" but "yes I will have a lemonade" came out instead. I had been sitting there all day like a wall flower praying for the moment that 'Sex on legs' would get me up to dance to Deirdre and 'Sexy Boy's' first dance and then we could slow dance to 'Lady in Red' by Chris De Burgh, even though she was in white, after all, this was the biggest hit of the year.

He had bright blue eyes and because he was a genuinely nice guy and so being Deirdre's wee sister, he did give me attention, obviously not the attention I wanted, but to me … he really liked me. To him though, I was just the wee sister. By this stage, I was fourteen and at the end of the day he was twenty four and I think that may have been the beginning of me fancying older men.

My parents were so proud that day and Mummy loved to dance and you would have seen her dancing around the floor with her female friends because that was a popular thing to do if you didn't have a dance partner and my Daddy wasn't a big dancer. I knew that a change was coming, because Deirdre was moving into her new home with her 'Sexy Boy' as a married woman.

There was that moment at the wedding where the music was playing loudly and there was a silence in my head. All I could see was everyone on the dance floor, Mr & Mrs 'Sexy Boy', Geraldine & her boyfriend, our Michael and Brendan, and all the extended friends and family. I then looked to the left of the dance floor and I noticed that Daddy had taken Mummy's hand and led her to the dance floor.

Everything went into slow motion, because he had got her up to dance and it was the happiest moment ever. I was so thrilled. It was just the most amazing moment of my life to date. I began imagining, this is how they must have looked when they danced on their own wedding day.

It was so lovely seeing them dancing around the dance floor like they did when they were young. Daddy hadn't danced in years and here he was the proud father of his eldest daughter on her wedding day and he was looking into my Mummy's eyes with pure love, both looking amazingly happy and proud. The dance seemed to go on forever. What a beautiful, beautiful moment.

Little did we know ….

Tragedy was just around the corner!

DIFFERENT

I don't remember much after Daddy died, everything changed.

One day a wedding, then a funeral
Mummy full of grief, she lost her best friend and husband
Me, my Daddy

He was tall dark and handsome
The perfect gent
I will always remember his bluey grey polo neck
That, I'll never forget

My sisters were married
One brother turned to booze, the other I really don't know
Me? I didn't want to show what I was feeling.

I spent nights alone in my bedroom
That's all I could do
I couldn't share the pain
Handle mine or anyone else's.

Things became so different
A happy family, then sad
But life goes on, or so they say
But mine became different
I began to hide my emotions more
Until one day I didn't feel anything

Pauline Carville

Dark clouds became my daily life
With no light at the end of the tunnel
I didn't know how I'd gotten there
I could see no way back and no way forward.

I shut my family out as much as I could
Then I felt awfully lonely
I looked for a guy to take daddy's place
Just a big mistake!

I am trying to be strong
But I can't see ahead, all I see is darkness
I am crippled with fear and a heaviness pounds against my
heart
It beats faster and faster everyday
I want to see clearly
I want to live again
I just want it to be the way I used to be.

Please help me, someone, Please?

CHAPTER 9 - DIFFERENT: EVERYTHING HAD CHANGED

So it was Saturday morning and Mummy hadn't been well all that week, she had really bad pains in her back which hadn't happened before. At the same time Daddy had been back at work and he just loved going to the Cooley Mountains at the weekend and normally Mummy and Daddy would go together to see their friends in Templetown.

This Saturday morning Daddy came into their bedroom, I was sitting on the bed beside Mummy as I had just made them both a cup of tea, this was a popular occurrence in our house, ever since I was able to boil the kettle and they wanted a cup of tea, everyone would sing "Polly put the kettle on" so I was doing my daughterly duty.

Daddy said "Sheila I am going to take a wee trip down to Templetown" That's where their friends lived.

Mummy said

"Awk Brendan, don't be going today"

I could see the disappointment in his face, he really wanted to go.

For the last year, maybe even longer when Daddy went to Templetown without mummy, my younger brother would go with him. Brendan was getting to the stage where he was starting to break away from the apron strings and wanted to gallivant with his friends. So when Daddy asked him if he wanted to go, Brendan declined.

I do remember mummy repeating "Awk Brendan, would you not just give it a miss today? I don't want you to go, I have a strange feeling" which is something mummy never would have said to him

Daddy said "Sheila, I will only be a couple of hours to get my head showered" (West Belfast for clearing his head)

So off he went after saying all his goodbyes. I remember that. We used to go as a family on a regular basis, but never had mummy ever asked him not to go. I think she just felt so unwell, maybe she wanted him to keep her company, but he had been working all week and just wanted a wee break.

I don't really remember much about that day and what I did. I do recall turning the chair that sat under the window facing the living room door all the way round to face the television which is what I did every Saturday night … to me, it was the best seat in the house. So as it was Saturday night, we were getting ready to watch a movie. Mummy sat on the sofa with her feet up and a blanket around her. We were watching "Two Minute Warning" (The Los Angeles Police Department, led by Capt. Peter Holly (Charlton Heston), learns that a madman is planning to open fire on a football pitch during a huge game). We were half way through the film when the phone rang…

Mummy answered …. I could tell by the silence and mummy's body language that something was wrong! When mummy came off the phone she instantly dialled my Aunt's number. Deirdre had just come back from her honeymoon and Geraldine and her boyfriend were spending the night at the newlywed's new house and they didn't have a phone.

I heard mummy say "There's something wrong with Brendan, they have found his car"

I began questioning mummy trying to get any information from her, she wasn't being very open in her responses which frustrated me and part of me was raging as I was enjoying this film and now something was interrupting it, I suppose you could say I was being a typical teenager, but mummy had mentioned a few times that daddy was late and was wondering what was keeping him.

What was usually a twenty minute car journey from East Belfast was done in what felt like a minute when my aunt and uncle were at the door. I now knew something serious was wrong because mummy practically collapsed with emotion into my aunt's arms.

My heart sank! I had never seen mummy react this way. I was petrified! Soon after, they left for the Police Station.

I was fourteen, I wanted to be an actress and at the same time I was trying to protect myself. So I began telling myself that if something was really wrong and of course I was thinking the worst, if daddy was dead (I never thought this could actually happen). I was afraid to stay positive in case the worst really did happen and I wouldn't be able to cope.

So I began to prepare myself and reassure the child within, that if something was wrong with daddy I could use it in my acting. I was just trying to make a positive out of the negative.

Something really was wrong. Mummy was going to Woodburn Police Station. Daddy was across the border, the Garda was now communicating with the Police and information was coming through slowly.

I was trying to put things together in my mind of what might have happened; I just felt this was easier than waiting to find out what was really going on.

When mummy came home and said that daddy was dead my arms and legs and whole body went completely numb. It was just as well, I was sitting down. I think at that moment I didn't really know what to do or say and I was in complete silence, sitting in shock. I could hear chatter around me, mummy crying like a banshee as you can imagine.

My older sisters were unreachable as they didn't have a phone in the house and of course in those days, there were no mobile phones and our Michael was out clubbing. Brendan was crying like a baby, Godlove him, me, I was still numb. You see I was now thinking that it was my fault. I had killed my daddy because earlier I had said to myself that if daddy was dead "I could use it in my acting", now I felt that I had wished him dead and blamed myself. From that moment I shut down completely.

I know the Police had to go to Deirdre's house, in Glengormley, to tell them what had happened and again it felt like a matter of minutes when they all finally walked in.

I couldn't show my feelings; I didn't actually feel a thing. If you can imagine, me thinking daddy was dead, I was hoping the news would be good news and that if it wasn't, it would help me, if I prepared for the worst, only now I was feeling like I had killed him by thinking he was dead.

I couldn't express anything, or feel anything, I couldn't put my arms around mummy to make her feel better or get support. I thought that this was my fault! I did this! I suppose as I think of it, I don't even think I was the type of person to put my arms around mummy anyway at that time. I wasn't like my older sisters or anyone in my family for that matter, I was different and I always knew it!

So when I saw Deirdre and Geraldine walk in and go straight to mummy and sat at either side of her, holding her and crying together, I was jealous, jealous that they were able to do that because I couldn't bring myself to. With the shock, I was now stuck in my own head.

After that I remember lots of people being at the house for the wake. A West Belfast wake is where the coffin would come to the house, opened, so that family and friends could come and pay their respects. Everyone in the neighbourhood arrived with sandwiches and cake, milk and sugar and all the necessities so that everyone was fed. There was so much food. Irish stew, lasagne, extra cups and saucers and the kettle was constantly on. It really was a time when our whole community really pulled together. I mean the house was full. People were coming from everywhere.

I had experienced death before when my Great Aunt Peg had died but I can't remember her funeral. This was the first death in the family that I remembered and it was my wee Daddy. I just couldn't believe this was happening to me, to us. I didn't want to see him in the coffin, because a few days before I had dreamt that daddy had died and was laying in a coffin, so was Mummy. There was another empty coffin waiting for me. Now I wasn't just getting weird warnings, now I was dreaming events and this had now taken place. It felt like I was seeing into the future and this really was sending me over the edge. Every time I closed my eyes I could see what my daddy was going to look like in the coffin. I did see him and my fear was confirmed, he looked exactly the same in my dream. This would now continue the nightmares that you could brush off as bad dreams, now my dreams were coming true and this developed the horror of going to sleep. Was I going to see my mummy die now? After all, she was also in my dream!

Unusual Circumstances

The Facts!

My Daddy was on his way back home from Temple Town and he was found in what was later described by the press as "Strange Circumstances" half way up Slieve Foye Forest Park, which is between Carlingford and Omeath...

Someone had been up in the forest and seen my Daddy there and had called the Guards, but the man didn't call the local guards in Carlingford; he rang the Dundalk Guards, which would have taken much longer to deal with the incident. This was very strange! The man did not want to be known and did not want the Guards to get there too quickly.

My Daddy was found lying outside his car, laid out like he was in a coffin ... naked, his clothes were folded, beside him. There was no evidence of foot prints or tyre prints and no evidence that anyone had been there. But someone was there!

It was ruled at the Inquest, that my Daddy had a massive heart attack and had a brain storm, hence why he was found up in the forest, as they believed he felt unwell and came off the road to die. It was ruled this way as there was insufficient evidence to rule anything else.

I know that someone caused my daddy to die that day! The man who called it into the Dundalk Guards was at the scene. Why? Yes Daddy had a heart attack but there was definitely more to it than that. I believe that someone my daddy knew took him off the road and something happened and instead of trying to get him to do something that he didn't want to do ….. He took a massive coronary and died. Why were there no footprints or tyre prints? Why did this man not try to help him?

So do I know something untoward happened to my Daddy? …. Absolutely. Can I prove it? ….. No!

I have resigned myself to the fact that nothing can ever bring daddy back!

Chapter 10 - After Daddy Died

After daddy died, it did change how I communicated, I must admit. I spent most of my days in my little box room, bedroom. It was my sanctuary away from everyone. I would sit there and cry. Yes I was crying, I just didn't let anyone see that. I also wrote in my diary to express every thought and emotion I had. This was the only way I could express it. I named my diary, Misty; this was because at this stage the low mood had a reason to be low. Everything had changed in our house. My eldest sister was married and left the home which left a big gap; five weeks later daddy was gone too.

I didn't want to talk about what happened with anyone and especially my Mummy (God love her) and she needed me so much but I had nothing in me. I just kept pushing everything down, acting as if everything was normal and my poor Mummy was so devastated. We were all getting to the age where she and Daddy would have had more time together and now he was gone. She was always trying to talk about it, which was the opposite of what I wanted to do, so that obviously affected our relationship back then.

Everyone knows that your Mummy is the best person to speak to when you are going through a hard time, but Mummy was also going through a difficult time and I regularly heard family members saying 'Keep up for your Mummy' in other words in my mind don't let Mummy know how you feel. So I did that and yet mummy knowing how I was feeling would have helped her, but I continued to keep my feelings inside, so much so that all my emotional reactions became aggressive. My mummy was the best person to speak to about

Daddy's death and anything for that matter which I realised when I returned home after living in Glasgow and London years later.

"Mummy this illness wasn't about daddy's death" I told her. She blamed herself on not getting me therapy at the time. Therapy was taboo then as well as mental illness, so I am not surprised.

I now realise that I could have saved myself the years of turmoil if I had just gone to mummy in the first place. She was totally the right person to talk to and she would have gotten me the help I needed and most importantly the support that was required. Instead I hid it, I pushed anything that had happened or didn't want to deal with deep down and blocked it out any way I could. This definitely made matters much, much worse. I continued to hide my truth, behind the façade that everything was well, it really wasn't!

CHAPTER 11 - MEN

I never seemed to have much luck with men

All my friends were dating, and successfully dating

Me, I just kept choosing the wrong ones.

My first real boyfriend was such a lovely guy. His father had been shot during the troubles in West Belfast hit as he was making his way home from work and I always really felt sorry for him. He was quite an emotional guy and very genuine and I always knew he was gay so I knew that wasn't going to work, however we did become great friends.

Then I met 'The Driver'. I call him that because he would drive all of us on a Friday or Saturday night to the disco at The Slieve Donard Hotel in New Castle, County Down or to Burberrys Disco, in Portrush, on the North Coast.

I went out with him for a year and on the year anniversary

He said

"Pauline, I think you are great and I know you inside out and upside down and there's nothing else to know"

Can you believe it? He knew me inside out and we didn't even have sex?

Anyway a few years later I hear he has eight kids.

Thank God he broke up with me eight kids? Definitely not my dream life!

My modelling career was going well when I met 'The Jealous & Possessive one'. I was doing extremely well as a model, but typical me, I picked another dud.

His name preceded him. It was my fault if another guy looked at me.

I must have been winking at every guy who passed us, to hear this guy

He wanted to know where I was, morning, noon and night and he even wanted me to take cooking lessons because he said his X could cook.

Then I got into West Side Story directed by Michael Poynor with Opera Northern Ireland. I was so excited, but sure didn't he start. He wasn't happy that I would have to get physically close to my male dance partner.

"I am not cheating, I am not cheating! It's Westside Fuckin Story for fucks sake. Not Westside Story come Orgy" Oh fuck off, you're doing my head in."

Needless to say we broke up. Little did he know that my dance partner was trying to tickle my fanny every single night on stage? Stupid Eejitt! (Irish for Idiot). Of course my dance partner got a good slap every night. Remember what the nuns said?

Michael Poynor spotted me during West Side Story miming to 'Love takes time' by Maria Carey in the rehearsal space when everyone was out for lunch. Even at this stage I needed to protect my head space so I stayed in this particular day so that I could calm my head down and get a little bit of space, before getting back to rehearsal. I was totally mortified when I heard someone clapping. It was Michael. He said "that was the best piece of acting that I have seen for a long time"

I laughed, I thought he was joking; he was perfectly serious and said that he would help me get into Drama School if that's what I wanted, after this show closed. Michael prepared me for all of my auditions and I will be forever grateful.

A monologue that I loved performing was from "The Woman Who Cooked Her Husband by Debbie Isitt. "I don't like being a woman" was the opening line and this was so apt at this time. I also used it for many auditions throughout my acting career and this piece also became a cathartic experience, especially when I had men troubles.

Am I Mad or What?

Pauline Carville

Modelling shot from 1992

Another modelling shot from back in the day

Pauline Carville

Style Academy portfolio 1991

Style Academy portfolio 1991

July 1990, about to go clubbing

The Original 'Woman Who Cooked Her Husband' Monologue

Laura: "I don't like being a woman - I don't like it!!! I don't like being banished to the kitchen at parties talking about stupid things with stupid females. I want to be where you are with the men all laughing and joking and drinking and smoking - I want to join in! I can't do the things you ask of me - I'm not like your other wife - I'm not cut out for household chores - I cannot stand the monotonous, endless routines, the mindless activities involved - who gives a fuck if the door knobs are't polished?! Why make the bed, just to sleep in it again - I can't see the point - it doesn't make sense! You do it if you want to - hire someone - hire Hilary - anything just to get the pressure off my back. I do my best for you, don't I? It's not like I'm lazy or stupid or incompetent - I starve myself for you - I try and get my fat bum down and my small tits up - I exercise! I know I'm no great cordon bleu chef but I have a go - the thanks I get. Have you any idea what it feels like to drool over cookbooks all day, fantasizing about delicious recipes that I'm not allowed to eat in case I get fat and even if I could eat them I couldn't fucking cook them for the life of me because I am so crap!"

From 'The Woman Who Cooked her Husband'
By Debbie Isitt

I also later used this monologue as inspiration to my version of why 'I don't like being a woman'.

I met 'The Jealous & Possessive' one in the Greenan Lodge

disco on a Friday night. We got serious very quickly and then suddenly, out of the blue he showed a side of himself I wasn't happy with. He didn't like the fact that I was in the newspapers and doing catwalk modelling in my underwear where men could look at me. He didn't want other men being able to look at me like that. Well this really pissed me off! My aim was not to be a model, I wanted to be an actor and if he didn't like me getting attention now, what was he going to be like when I was on stage or television doing love scenes? So this was certainly going to be a problem.

Within six months he was trying to control my every move. He even tried to make me feel like I was going mad when he told me that he had seen me kissing another man in the Crown Bar, when I was there doing a drinks promotion. I would go through every minute of the night in my head like a movie. I knew I hadn't kissed anyone, why would I? I was working, besides cheating wasn't in my DNA. His plan worked though, I was second guessing myself all the time.

He was two years older than me and he had been on a year out from University in London and that year had come to an end. He went back to London and I was due to start a new drinks campaign with Bacardi which was worth a lot of money to me. I left my office job at 5 O'clock and walked out onto Howard Street in Belfast and I thought I was seeing things. He had just left two days before and there he was standing on the sidewalk with a very strange look on his face.

I lost that Bacardi job because of him. He had me in such a state that when I called the Agency they were not a bit happy that I couldn't go to work that night. This wasn't just a boyfriend issue, this was a depression issue which comes clear later. Not long after this I broke up with him.

I'd better tell you about my modelling days.

There were very few opportunities to perform and by this stage I was working with our Deirdre in a Solicitors Office.

You have to understand that I was a creative person, I was really serious about being an actor and at this time there was very little here, so you can imagine that a dream like this really did appear to be a dream. It was sensible to get a normal job, and that is what I did.

I was completely and utterly bored out of my mind. I was still holding onto that dream, then I realised that I had to find other ways to perform. I was tall, five foot nine, thin, and not bad looking and decided that I would look into modelling. Style Academy was in their infancy. I was tall enough to do the catwalk and the personality and I suppose the fun loving part of me that would work for promotional jobs.. Now I was represented by the Agency and modelling is what I started to do.

Back then promotion work was paid really, really well and I worked a lot and made some great friends within the agency and I loved it because I had the opportunities to be seen, to be photographed, to perform and really it was my social life as well.

I did catwalks with Geoff Banks for Northern Ireland Hairdressing Awards and lots of drinks campaigns. As I was a performer I was getting other opportunities too. I got dance promotions and became a regular dancer in the Manhattan Club that became the M Club.

Cool FM's John Kearns knew my modelling agent and through her, I became the backing vocalist for John's band. The song was a popular release "Shake Yourself" which was played all the time on the radio back then.

So you can see that I was modelling, dancing and singing, and performing professionally was at the forefront of my mind and I took every opportunity to do that.

By now I was a very successful model, working in the solicitor's office, working as a dancer on the weekends, I never stopped really. My brothers used to call me "The Bank of Ireland". I probably had more money back then, than I do now.

So you can imagine when I lost work at the agency because of 'The Jealous & Possessive One', I was totally gutted.

Awk it wasn't all bad in terms of my experience with men. I did have fun sometimes, if I allowed myself and one day at college. I let my guard down.

Suddenly I see him.....

'The Scot'! Well I was in Scotland at the time.

Oh, he was beautiful and for the first time in a long time a guy was actually interested in me and the feeling was mutual.

Every time he talked to me, I got all flustered and I felt like I couldn't speak properly. I probably looked like a complete dick. We were good friends too and I thought we shouldn't really take it any further.

So I kissed him a couple of times

Then one night, we had a couple of glasses of wine and I was wearing my new black jeans

No, no, trying to contain myself and be the good girl

No I'm not having sex with you. If you're just here for sex you can get out.

What do you mean do I like you? Of course I like you. Oh fuck off, you're doing my head in.

A few nights later, we had a couple of glasses of wine again!

We ended up back at mine.... in bed. Do you think I had sex with him?

When I walked into college the next day, I could feel the red flush come up my neck. It was him. He gave me a knowing smile....

And all I could see was his .... !

There was so much drama around men; I decided to focus on my career!

Right! That's it! NO MORE MEN!

This is when I decided to write my version of the monologue in 'The Woman Who Cooked Her Husband' By Debbie Isitt

I Don't Like Being A Woman - My Version

I don't like being a woman
I really don't like it
I want to be a man having a laugh and a geg about whatever
they seem to have a wee geg about.

I want to worry only about what I'm gonna put in my mouth
next and I mean food
(You have dirty minds)

Cause to a man all they seem to think about is eating and
sleeping and then eating and sleeping again oh and eat sleep
and shitting.

I can't be the way they want me to be!
I need someone who will understand me when I don't
understand myself.
I want a man to comfort me when I'm feeling low.
I want someone to make me laugh when I'm stressed
Or tell me I'm beautiful, when I feel ugly.
Instead, I seem to choose the man who tells me I'm ugly
when I feel beautiful
And totally shatters any Self Esteem I had to begin with.

Is there something wrong with me?
I keep repeating the same mistake over and over.
It's like I am torturing myself and I don't know how to stop.

By Pauline Carville
Inspired by 'The Woman Who Cooked Her Husband'
By Debbie Isitt

I soon realised when I know what I don't want it is easier for me to work out what I do want and this has become a mantra that I have used ever since.

Chapter 12 - The Clouds: When Did It All Start?

I have to admit when I got to this point in writing about my depressive days I have found it very difficult to face, not because I don't want to talk about it, but more about the fact that I don't want to put myself back in that state. It was a very debilitating time for me. Back in 2011 I did the play version of "Am I mad or what" and I did knock myself into a very deep depression which affected me for a number of years where I was unable to work again. So you can understand why I found this part difficult, even though this is the whole point. I think I have spent a lot of time avoiding this particular chapter, even though I have been sharing some of my poetry at that time.

Therapy

Therapist – When is your first memory of feeling this low?

It all started to get really bad ….. I suppose I had low times in my teens, you know, of course you could say I felt low after my Daddy died because things were different, everything had changed. Did I believe that the dark clouds, the fog, the feelings, the deep routed feelings that I was experiencing, when I felt suicidal came from the fact that my father had died? The answer was definitely no! I couldn't tell why I was feeling that way. I certainly knew when a therapist said "Oh! You didn't cry when your daddy died? Well that is why you are feeling this way, when you don't express emotion at a trauma, it will come out sometime, in a different form, this is it"

Our family doctor had told my Mummy that it would come out sometime, however the Doctors and Counsellors were all trying to pin what was happening for me, was the fact that my Daddy died when I was fourteen in suspicious circumstances and deep down, I knew that was not what was happening. I just knew in my gut, I didn't know why I felt this way, I just did.

So how did I feel? I had circling thoughts, dark thoughts, why am I here? What is the point? Who really cares about me? I am an awful person, I am no good at anything, nobody likes me, and no one wants to be around me. If they knew what I was thinking and feeling they definitely wouldn't want to be around me. Yet I used to be a happy go lucky person or so I thought. I suppose I could question that now. Was I always acting? Was I pretending that I was happy? That in a way was my front to disguise what I was feeling and making everyone believe that I was ok. When I look back over different stages in my life I did pretend that I was ok. But I wasn't!

It was a feeling that when I woke up in the morning I felt like I was sinking into the bed and through the floor. That is how low I felt. I didn't want to get up. I didn't feel like I had anything to get up for. Every thought I had was dark and it circled round and round. I did try to change the thoughts to positive thoughts but I felt like I had no control over them and so my daily life was a complete struggle. I became so desperate for help and this was just at the beginning when I was still living at home.

I did go to a GP in our Doctors Surgery, I avoided of course going to my Mummy's GP as I was afraid that he would tell her, and that would worry her and that was the last thing I wanted to do. So I went to a different one. She said "You are in the middle of a breakup with your boyfriend, this will pass" I knew that it wasn't about him either. I had been feeling this way since I was 15, already 6 years.

There was no definite reason behind these 'Clouds' that I began to call them because I didn't know it was called Depression. I hadn't heard that word before and everything else in my life was going really well.

I remember getting my big break as a model when I was 19 working for Style Academy, this was a new modelling agency and I was doing lots of big jobs including CatWalk Shows, lots and lots of promotional work, drinks promotions including Budweiser, Sambuca & Baileys, Bacardi, Martini, gosh I remember the Martini gig we were on roller boots serving Martini to anyone passing the front of the City Hall. I was regularly the fashion Model for the Sunday World with photographer Alwyn James. I was getting my picture taken and filmed on a regular basis for different events; I was even on the very popular UTV show "Ask Anne " with the lovely Anne Hailes who is now a really good friend of mine. .

Even though all this was going on, to the public and my modelling friends and my family, I was as happy as Larry' (another Belfast saying when I was younger) I was struggling with these deep dark thoughts and my confidence levels were at an all time low.

I had taken and put into practice a lot of the advice that I was given, go out walking, go to the gym so that you can focus on something other than the terrible thoughts and crippling feelings and that did pull me out of some bouts of the depression from the age of fifteen to now at age 21, but this felt different now.

I mean when it started really badly I was going out with The Jealous & Possessive One and the relationship was not going very well, but I also knew at that time that the stuff that was currently going on wasn't necessarily about my boyfriend. Yes he was possessive and jealous and caused me some stress, but there was more to it …. And I knew it.

As I mentioned I was working with Style Academy and it was the second modelling agency that I knew of in Belfast other than Alison Campbell Agency (ACA). I was so excited to be there and something within me gave me the get up and go and the determination to actually go to the Agency, however in the back of my mind I was waiting for the knock back thinking that no one would want me. There clearly was something deep within me that believed that I was worth the effort. Otherwise, how could I have applied for these opportunities and go for the auditions that came up? Otherwise why would you put yourself out as a model? Although my main aim there was to perform in whatever way I could as there wasn't much acting happening here back then.

I remember going to the Style Academy office after about a year of working with them to discuss a job or rehearse a Catwalk show and I would go in with my face on both with full make up and the smile I would show on my face, I suppose you could say that character that I portrayed in front of everyone and then I walked out of the office on the Holywood Road and I stood at the edge of the road blankly staring and thinking that if I walked across this road and was knocked down and died, would it really matter? I just felt that low within myself and it was exhausting to act like I was ok on a daily basis. I suppose that was another reason to want to get knocked down. For all I was thinking ….. Please just stop!

A car pumped its horn to get my attention, little did they know that this was truly the first time I felt suicidal and yet I was so successful. I was making a great living from modelling and dancing, I also worked in a Solicitors office with my sister and River Island. I was doing all the things the doctor had said to do and still I was at rock bottom.

On a bad day

CHAPTER 13 - MY SCOTTISH ADVENTURE

Leaving home for the first time I must say was difficult in one sense and a relief on the other. I felt guilty leaving Mummy on her own and although she had Michael and Brendan at home with her, I knew she would miss me as she had begun relying on my company after Geraldine got married.

I remember seeing tears in her eyes (my wee Mummy) trying her best to be strong and to make me believe that she was ok with me leaving. I knew she was really proud.

I must admit though, leaving Belfast in the early nineties was a relief to me also. Getting away from what I believed was torture of both news channels on a daily basis to get both versions of the news that my Mummy would watch daily. 'The troubles' were still going on. That underlying tension in the air that anyone living in Belfast would feel. So you can imagine to my surprise when I first moved to Glasgow and people asked

"What part of Belfast are you from?

I would answer in an abrupt manner.

"Why? Do you know Belfast?

I was in Scotland to train in acting at the (RSAMD) Royal Scottish Academy of Music & Drama (renamed today to (RCS) Royal Conservatoire of Scotland and I was not going to have those questions following me to my new life in Scotland. Of course I learnt quickly that those questions were in relation to football, Celtic and Rangers. Again – not interested!

I was well organised for the move to Scotland and even had a room booked in a house in close proximity to the college for two weeks before starting so that I could investigate the best areas close to the college and then, I could find something on a more permanent basis.

I was greeted by the lady of the house who showed me around and then to the room I would be staying in and she proceeded to tell me that if I needed anything ... to ring the servants bell.

"The servant's bell? Where have I walked into I thought?

Upstairs, Downstairs?"

I have to say, I didn't feel very comfortable and the bathroom was at the other end of the hall near to the room where the Lord and Lady of The Manor slept, if you get my drift?

Well, I was only going to be there for two weeks and as I had paid for the room in advance I thought

"You have to suck it up Pauline"

I used the bathroom to do my daily night time routine and I settled into bed at 10pm. What else was there to do? There was no television and I suppose I was pretty tired after all the travelling and nervous energy I had used throughout the day.

I began tossing and turning and sleep didn't come easily as I had now begun to worry about needing the toilet during the night and waking the household.

By the time it got to 1am, I was now genuinely needing the loo and so persuaded myself to get up and go to the door. It was one of those old doors with a round handle that you had to turn and pull at the same time.

So I grabbed the handle and it came off in my hand. I tried to fix it back into the hole it came out of but it didn't open.

Oh no ... I was locked in!

"Oh leave it to me. I have broken the bloody door"

I had tried pushing it into the hole it came out of, it did go in but it wouldn't turn.

"Oh God" ...

I really was locked in!

I spent the next hour or so walking up and down trying to decide if I should call the servants bell. No, this was out of the question. I was so scundered! (Belfast for embarrassment). There was no way I was pulling that bell rope. But what was I going to do? I began looking around the room for a bin or something that I could pee in ... still there was nothing.

By now I was doubled over, absolutely dying to go to the loo, it was now 5am, four hours later. Bearing in mind I was literally about to wet myself and now realised that it was now definitely too late to ring the damn bell.

So, desperate times, calls for desperate measures. There was nothing else for it. I was going to have to climb out through the window, onto the roof, jump and then let myself in through the front door with my key.

So without delay, I pushed open the window and began the climb. You might think I was mad at this point, believe me I did, but there was nothing else I could do. Well, I suppose I could have pee'd from the roof, but then I was concerned that the lady would smell the pee on the patio in the morning. Yes I was now thinking about this as I stood on the roof in my P.J.'s, but this indeed was the least of my problems.

Suddenly I heard the back door open. Oh no the man of the house had heard something on the roof and now there he was looking up at me.

"What are you doing?"

What was I supposed to say? "Oh Jesus Christ if you could get a hole to swallow me whole right now I would be grateful"

I very quickly explained what had happened while he got me a ladder so that I could climb down.

His response was ...

"Why didn't you ring the servant's bell?"

(The servant's fucking bell?) I thought. Then said "I was afraid to wake you?"

Here I was, having done precisely that!

When I got down from the roof I apologised profusely.

"I am so sorry I was just dying to go to the toilet"

He said "It's ok. Don't worry"

"But I am worried" I said "Do you think I am mad or what?

In terms of what just happened? You can imagine his response!

It was time to move!

When I started at Drama School, I was introduced to another Irish Actor from Keady, County Armagh who also had a room available for rent which was not only down the street from the School, she had trained there too.

Of course I jumped at the chance after seeing it. It was this amazingly large flat on Sauchiehall Street at Charing Cross.. I was also thrilled when I heard another actor – Louise who also trained at the Conservatoire was also moving in. Things were looking up.

The day I moved in, I met the other housemate Bruce, I did feel for him though. "Three actors and an Accountant" (I could make this into a movie). He was so quiet and reserved, then there was us, "The Three Degrees'' so different in many ways and yet similar as we all shared one passion – Acting!

Veronica (Ronnie) and Louise (Lou), we had really hit it off from day one and have some great memories. Lou really took me under her wing. I think she really understood that I was struggling and she had such compassion.

Finally I could talk to someone who was not at all judging me. She also realised quickly that I needed a life outside of the madness of Drama School and that is when she began inviting me out with her to theatre shows and her Friday night events all over the city of Glasgow and sometimes we would venture to Edinburgh along with her fantastic group of friends.

I finally felt really wanted and for the first time in Glasgow I felt like I really fitted in. Lou was like family to me. She really cared. So much so that when my Mummy would visit and I was at college during the day, Lou would look after her, take her shopping, go for lunch and keep her company until I got home. She was even my mummy's plus one at my Royal Conservatoire Graduation which meant so much to me .... and my Mummy.

I worked in a very popular fashion store, throughout my years in Glasgow and had great friends there too. There was always someone in the shop on a Saturday telling me where the party that night would be, which was always in the flat of someone I worked with.

The Glasgow Parties were Epic!

The preparation for those was done with precision. Everything had to be ready – and I don't mean the food! I am talking about the wine, the beer, the spirits and its mixers. Wine in Tesco back then was only £2.99 a bottle so affordability for all. You could spend £20 for a good night– and that was just the beginning.

An essential part of these parties would be ... Drugs!

Don't worry, there was no way I would have been taking drugs. Was I not mad enough? Knowing my luck, something that could make most, have an amazing high, would more than likely do the opposite for me.

Cocaine was a popular drug of choice in Glasgow (if you had the money to buy it or didn't end up hanging over the toilet boking if it was too much for you) I saw that alot. The cheaper high was E tabs which were still around. Then there was the daily drug of choice for my shop worker friends – Maruana Joints – the very fact I give the drug its full title shows I wasn't experienced in these matters.

However, one Saturday, my friend from work, Marie and I went back to her flat. I was so weary and tired and couldn't wait to sit down to a glass of wine. It was her turn to host the party that night.

I jumped into the shower first and when I walked into the kitchen with the towel over my head, she was sitting, rolling joints which looked like we were having a joint convention. There were so many. She was getting ready for our big party..

I was fascinated by now and poured myself a glass of my £2.99 a bottle vino that had been chilling quickly in the freezer and said

"I will help you. Show me what to do"

So while she got ready, I was rolling these joints. It took a while for my fingers to get into the flow and the more I rolled the more intrigued I became.

"This must be good," I thought.

After getting my glad rags on I asked her if I could try. Well everyone was clearly going to be having a great time, there was enough there to last a month!

"Am I missing out?"

So I took the plunge and took my first draw ... nothing.

Even the second and the third one had no effect, so the next draw was big. Oh yes and then suddenly without realising, I was telling the best story you have ever heard, only I couldn't seem to get past the first line. So I kept going back to the start again and again and then suddenly ...

The giggling began. Everything that she said I would burst out laughing, everything made me laugh particularly when our first guest arrived, Sharon.

Marie had not been brought up in any way religious and she was intrigued to hear what it was like to go into a confessional and confess your sins. She kept asking me what it was like.

It's funny what people do. So I set up the confessional – the hall cupboard!

Inside our 'Confessional Cupboard' was Marie, she was there to watch and learn. As I was an Actor in training I got to play the Priest. Poor Sharon had no choice as no one else had arrived yet and of course we were high and thought this was hilarious.

To begin with, I had to go through the process of the confessional with Sharon and I wanted to give Marie an authentic experience so I did this whilst Marie sat in the cupboard waiting for us to enter. I had made it very clear to Sharon that going to confess your sins was a very serious spiritual experience so they both really had to believe that this was real so that they both got as real an experience as possible.

How I kept a straight face at the time, I don't know as Marie and Sharon were so focused and I had given Sharon the opening line that she needed to start her Confession.

The cupboard was dark except for the candle that Marie was holding so we could see a little, as well as the candle that I had in my left hand to light my face. When I think of it, candles inside the hall cupboard filled with coats, the ironing board and hoover those candles could have caught fire. God knows what would have happened.

Anyway Sharon began to bless herself with the wrong hand. That is when I wanted to laugh quietly because she was now taking this so seriously. Afterall I had told her that she could be haunted by Priests that had already died who would watch over someone being blasphemous.

To begin with Sharon was confessing to taking an extra five minutes on her tea break in the shop that day, or for cursing in front of her little sister on a Sunday and being cheeky to her mummy the last time she visited.

That is when the Priest (me) asked her if there was anything else that was bothering her that she needed to get off her chest. That is when Sharon began to confess sins that neither Marie or I knew about.

The atmosphere in our makeshift confessional was now so serious, you could hear a pin drop. She began telling us that she didn't want to be with her boyfriend anymore and Marie and I looked at eachother thinking to ourselves is she making this up or is this real. I thought, here, Sharon is really good at this acting lark. So we stayed as serious as we could until she said in her strong Glaswegian accent

"Father, what do you think I should do? We just don't appear to be having much sex, do you think thats a problem?"

Was she serious, because he would be arriving soon for the party?

Oh my God, all three of us burst out laughing, remember I had done really well on this dope not laughing, considering before we entered the cupboard I had my first draws, even the doorbell ringing had made me laugh or the sound of the wine gurgling as I poured it into the glass.

Wow! Sharon had suspended her disbelief when she walked in and got so into it, she felt like she was actually in confession. However, she was telling the truth. She realised that although it started off as a laugh trying this religious ritual out, that we had created such a realistic scenario, that she felt able to confess. Don't worry she was so relieved that she had said it out loud that she was in stitches herself. We three girls were all glammed up ready for a party and suddenly we were all doubled over holding on to our crotches in case we wet ourselves laughing.

This had to be one of the best nights of my life and the party hadn't even begun.

Within an hour the flat was buzzing. Lots of laughter, chatter and lots and lots of dancing. I remember jumping up and down to Pulps 'Disco 2000' through to singing loudly to 'You Oughta Know' Alanis Morisette and as the night wound down there was always someone playing guitar singing Oasis 'Wonderwall' that album had recently been released and was huge.

The giggling would have stopped by now and my glazed eyes would have beer glasses on thinking how sexy the singer was. Of course the next morning I was extremely grateful that I didn't go there!

I had such an amazing night and that was the only joint I had that night and boy did it give me a much needed break from my own head. I was thinking if taking drugs makes me feel this good, why wouldn't I keep taking it? So for the next five Saturday nights after, I took a wee joint. I was getting a welcome break. I now realise why it was so popular.

Then my Birthday arrived and I was given a Psychic reading as a present. I was so excited. I was hoping she would tell me some positive news that could give me some hope.

When I walked into the stall that was in the corner of the shopping centre across the road from college, where its only privacy was a curtain this woman immediately said

"Stop smoking!"

"I don't smoke" I said

"You do, the wacky backy. You are a singer. You need your voice because London is beckoning you. I see you on a big stage with bright lights, singing! So do you hear me? Stop the wacky backy!

Oh my, I couldn't believe she could see this. Considering I wanted to sing, perform on the West End. Here she was telling me that I was going to do just that. For me this was a no brainer. I never smoked a joint again!

Although I took every opportunity to have a life away from college and the drama that drama students can't help but create. You know, "it's all about the drama". I did have some great friends who became very important to me during some of my most difficult times.

I was going into the Counsellors office on a daily basis as the clouds were following me every waking moment. I would get so stressed about exams or any written assignments that we had. That feeling of not being good enough, or not clever enough was constantly in the forefront of my mind and although we would only have one or two written assignments per term this would be a process of two weeks of heightened anxiety. Until two of my friends Rob and Leenie asked me if I would be interested in being part of the student Council. I couldn't believe they wanted me? This was such an important opportunity for me, not only did they appreciate me, they were trying to get me to realise what I had to offer.

The said "You are a director, you are business minded, a great organiser and you are so good with people"

I don't think they realised that they had just given me a lifeline.

We had our own little office to organise student events including Agent showcases. This also became a place where Leenie started to help me with my written Assignments. She realised that I had all the information needed in my head and could have an intelligent conversation about it, but because of a belief system that had been there since childhood. I believed I couldn't put the information on paper. That's when Leenie recorded us talking and then said

"Listen back to that ... Your assignment is now done!

I will be forever thankful to Leenie and Rob for always being there for me.

Other friends I will never forget from my Glasgow days Lyndsay and Gavin. They were in a relationship for over a year, in the last year of our course. I loved them. We had great chats and I would regularly go to theirs for dinner throughout this year. I was so gutted when they broke up. I had to adapt to seeing them separately and of course I did.

Both Lyndsay and Gavin became my confidants in the last months in Glasgow. Gavin would listen to my fears of leaving Glasgow and having to start again in London, whilst Lyndsay became my Acting Coach, working with me on my chosen monologues and songs for my audition into The Royal Academy of Music. Lyndsay helped me get my place there and without her, I wouldn't be where I am today. We lost contact and I can't remember how or why and I always worry about that because I can't remember what happened. Depression does that ... memory loss.

I have tried to contact Lyndsay through social media, to no avail and would love to get a chance to speak with her again and thank her. Maybe she got married or something. All I know is that part of my development from the clouds is to get closure on relationships or situations that cause anxiety or worry and I know not being able to talk to Lyndsay so that she can shed light on how and why we lost touch is so important.. Did I say or do something to offend her? I don't know. This is something that still to this day plays on my mind and if Lyndsay is reading this, I need her to know I will be forever grateful to her and I will always be in her debt.

It would mean the world to me to be able to make that connection with Lyndsay again!

DIARY ENTRY: 3RD FEBRUARY 1995

Oh Misty

I have been in such a bad place today. Every time someone even looked at me my eyes filled up. I really found it hard to get out of bed. As soon as I woke up I had that pins and needle feeling in my arms and I knew the clouds were still here. I don't know why I ever expect them to stop. I suppose I just think of a new day, maybe something may have switched during the night. I just have a nervous feeling all the time.

What is wrong with me? Why is this happening to me?

I think all I want to do is never get up again. That's how I feel but the last thing I want is for these feelings to stop me from my dream of being an actor, so I have to make myself get up each day. Being at drama school, I just want to be able to enjoy the process. Everyone is so upbeat and the competitiveness is rife. I really feel like I have to keep this to myself.

Everything is going round in my head over and over. Anything someone says or everything I say, I just feel like I am second guessing myself all the time. I am so afraid that if someone finds out I feel this way they won't let me finish my course and that everything is going to end.

What is wrong with me?

Oh God, please help me through these dark days, I feel like I am getting worse instead of better. I saw the counsellor today and I think she even thinks I am mad. I just need someone to help me!

Please I am desperate....

(Misty - The name I gave my diary when I began writing down my feelings, you could say she was my inner child I was talking to).

I was in my first year at The Royal Conservatoire of Scotland.

My acting headshot from 1998

Modelling in Glasgow in 1997

1997 Graduating from RCS. Rob Gallagher, Pauline, Lindsay Brown & Gavin Sinclair

1997 Graduation with Mummy & Louise Ludgate

Chapter 14 - How Did The Depression Manifest Itself

When I think of depression I don't just think of the very dark days in the end when I was suicidal, I actually think of the times that lead up to that. On many occasions my deep depression began with a lack of confidence in myself but also sudden days when I just didn't feel good. My mood was low, I felt fearful, confused and worried I suppose. That's how I would describe the beginnings of what later became known as The Clouds.

You have to remember I didn't have the word depression in my vocabulary. I didn't know that word; I hadn't even heard that word. To me I was just not feeling myself and of course that started to manifest itself in different ways.

First of all I started praying a lot, I was brought up as a Catholic and I believed and had been brought up to understand that if I prayed, God would take all that away. So my first experience of low mood and after keeping it a secret and not talking to anyone, not even my friends about it, I turned to God and the Church. That was my first experience of being obsessive. I started going to church before I went to work in the mornings, I would walk from home in West Belfast to St. Michael's on Finaghy Road North which was a couple of miles every morning, of course praying all the way there.

Please God help me

Please God I don't want to feel this way

Please help me to get out of this mood. What is wrong with me?

I would then kneel at the altar for an hour religiously saying prayers over and over again and also speaking to God like he was in the room with me because no one else knew about this and at this stage I needed to get what I was thinking and feeling out of my head. I would leave the house at 6.45am and not be at work until 9.00am. Then I would go to work and as the weeks went on of obsessively praying it came to the point where I couldn't do my next bit of work without praying so many times, repeating the prayer over and over until I felt I had said it with enough feeling, said it so that God had heard me, said it well enough so that God would see that I deserved help. I would also be crying and would have to repeat, repeat, repeat and even when I fulfilled all the rules I had put in place the obsession became more exaggerated, then I would have to get stronger in my interpretation or determination in the way I was saying it until I could concentrate on the next bit of work I had to do. So it was starting to affect my every waking moment.

After work, I would get off the bus at St. Michaels Church and kneel again for another hour until I could get up and go home, bearing in mind I had to keep an eye on the time as I was keeping it from my Mummy, no one knew I was doing this. Then I would walk back home again. That was another way of this low mood and not feeling good, this down feeling if you like because I didn't have any other words to describe it and that is why I started to give it a name … how I was feeling …. The Clouds.

The positive side of this obsessiveness is that I asked for positive things to happen so you could call it, well what I understand the name for it today is an affirmation. The affirmation was

"I am strong, confident and determined" I was saying it as if it was already happening even though I did not feel strong or confident, yes I was determined to stop feeling this way and with that I was willing to try anything to feel better. These were the words that motivated me to keep going. Of course I really must have had an inner strength deep down inside to enable me to keep going. I would be saying all this in my head and out loud so it wasn't just a silent affirmation. I said it out loud so that I could hear it. I really wanted to be strong, confident and determined because I didn't want the clouds to stand in my way and I knew I needed these qualities to move forward. There was an incredibly big fear that the men in the white coats would come and get me and my life would be over because I wasn't able to get the life that I wanted, so much.

Another part of chronic low mood and the feeling of despair is a very deep loneliness. Of course I was hiding this from everyone I knew because I was afraid that it would be confirmed that I was mental. So the loneliness exacerbated the obsessive behaviour, the praying and talking to myself. I needed to tell someone and I tried so hard to understand and logicalise what was happening to me and that is where the repetitiveness came from repeating, repeating, repeating my own explanation of what I was going through. It got to the point where if I didn't say the prayer or my own explanation the right way I would have to start from the beginning again. It's a bit like someone with Obsessive Compulsive Disorder where someone may have to turn the light switch on and off, on and off so many times until their brain realises they have done enough. Although OCD wasn't a condition that I had heard of either making what was happening extremely scary.

Although I never was diagnosed with OCD, this was just another manifestation of The Clouds. This went on for over 15 years.

You are probably wondering why this carried on for so long but the truth is I did go to the local GP in Belfast. I saw 3 different doctors in the surgery and they all came up with some reason that I was not feeling well. Break up from a boyfriend or what happened with daddy. I knew myself and I knew that none of these reasons made sense to me. It was like it was so deep, so hidden because that is what I had done for so long. They would suggest grief counselling or general counselling to alleviate these dark moods. They also suggested the gym which became another obsession because I did find that when I went to the gym every day for two weeks the mood did lift in the beginning. Funny I never got obsessed with alcohol or drugs, I was sensible enough to realise this would make things much worse and my reactions were severe enough.

I can't even explain how different I felt when I was able to lift myself out of the clouds. I would no longer have pins and needles, a lump in my throat, my heart racing, my mind circling and that awful feeling in the pit of my stomach that something bad was going to happen.

This continued when I was at The Royal Conservatoire of Music & Drama so I felt like I had been living this miserable existence longer than I had felt normal. The gym was no longer working and the obsessions, the low mood, the thoughts circling were now heightened. I wanted to bash my head against a wall to get it to stop. At Drama school it got really bad. I found it really hard to concentrate on anything other than the thoughts in my head. Concentration was a huge issue. Eventually I was crying all the time. It was like I was totally out of control. I don't know what everyone in my class must have thought. Yet there was something in me that was strong enough to know that I was good enough otherwise I wouldn't have been able to keep going and graduate which I did in 1997.

I found it difficult to be around people at college. I had a deep empathy for others, I was understanding, I had a sixth sense, I had a real connection to emotion hence actor training, so of course that would then affect me even more due to the fact that my emotions were all over the ,add someone else's anxiety, stress or sadness then I was going deeper and deeper into the clouds only now I was even more confused as I was now dealing with other people's shit as well as my own.

I had no alternative but to separate myself from the group so that I wasn't hearing the chitter, chatter or the jealousy and so because of this I became even more lonely. I had to physically separate myself from others and believe me I was always such a fun person I found this so difficult and yet knew I had no choice other than protect myself. I felt like I really was in danger territory. I was becoming paranoid and began having thoughts that I knew I shouldn't be having. Dark suicidal thoughts. What was happening to me? Why was this happening to me?

I still hadn't been able to tell anyone what was happening to me because I couldn't understand it myself. I just knew I wasn't well. This is when I became overcome with anxiety. I had been shaking inside my body. Now I was shaking physically and when I regularly became aware of the physical implications of what was happening to me I would cry uncontrollably trying to explain what was happening. However nothing made any sense.

I really wanted to connect with people and now The Clouds were really stopping me in every area of my life. I spent the first year of Drama School secretly going in and out of the counsellor's office. My biggest fear was that I would be asked to leave because I wasn't well.

The pressure of drama school also added to this as you are delving into your emotions, into who you are, positive attributes, your negatives so I needed respite at the end of the day I needed as much quiet time, alone time as I could. Of course drama school is not like university. It is full of classes then rehearsals from 9am to 9pm constantly learning new material and that is when I noticed that now the clouds were affecting my memory. Memorising lines was an integral part of an actor's work for crying out loud.

So at the end of a day and at the weekends I spent time trying to clear my head so that I was ready to start the process all over again on Monday. So I spent nights walking around Glasgow and the same when I was at the Royal Academy of Music in London, this was to stop me from thinking, getting a rest from my own head. I would hear people laughing and singing coming out of the bars or the cinema. There would be a lovely atmosphere in the air that would make me feel less lonely.

Going to the cinema was another way to rest my mind. I would go to a late show and watching someone else's story took my mind off mine. Although the mantras would come back, the repeating of the prayers, talking to myself that I can watch the film and let my head rest for a while and yet the voice in my head was constantly saying that I didn't deserve to watch this film, I didn't deserve anything good in my life. Thankfully I wasn't hearing voices, it was later explained that it was my subconscious.

What I am saying is that depression isn't just feeling low it also includes tiredness, loneliness, anxiety, memory loss, lack of concentration, feeling fearful constantly, lack of confidence, the headaches, the tiredness, oh the tiredness I was just so exhausted. I was exhausted because all of this is exhausting on its own but on top of that I just couldn't sleep. Sleep deprivation is a condition on its own; add that to the clouds, the depression and anxiety you now have desperation. I needed this to stop! This went on for years and years it is not surprising I became suicidal!

I always knew that there was something very wrong. I didn't know if it was just part of me or who I was or that it was just unfortunate that I was mental. I just had been so scared that I had to live like this for the rest of my life.

 I just wish now that I had talked to someone, anyone at the beginning. My mummy was the best person to speak to in the end and yet I was trying to protect her from all of this and in fact she was the person who could have helped me all along. Had I told her and gone to her own GP he would have given me medication the very first time I had experienced the deep depression and within six months I would have come through it. Instead I suffered for 15 years until I couldn't go on any longer. The breakdown began and as if that wasn't bad enough it took 10 years to get over that. So most of my life I was crippled with these clouds, that condition that begins with the word depression which I avoid using as a word now unless I really do feel depressed. I definitely do not deny how I am feeling anymore as that is detrimental to my mental health.

So if you recognise any of the above feelings or are suffering in silence please don't there is lots of support out there now.

So please do pick up the phone and tell someone you need help!

THE CLOUDS & ME #2

Clouds are hanging over me once more

Feelings of anxiety
Tears fall uncontrollably
Full of pain, NO, NOT AGAIN

The clouds and me
Will I ever be free of this darkness day and night?
Will it ever go away?

It's not as bad as it was before
Maybe if I just be patient I will be happy once more?
I know that you are listening to my quest
Very soon will I get my rest?

Chapter 15 - Talent & The Royal Academy Of Music

When I was in my third year at The Royal Conservatoire of Scotland I had the chance to sing for the West End Guru of Musical Theatre, Singing Teacher & Vocal Coach Mary Hammond and Founding Head of Musical Theatre at The Royal Academy of Music, London. Mary has worked with most of the Shows currently on the West End including Les Miserable, Miss Saigon (my favourite), Cats, Billy Elliot and Phantom of the Opera , The Witches of Eastwick, Starlight Express, Mama Mia and Cabaret. She has also worked with world renowned artists and bands including ColdPlay, Kaiser Chiefs, Muse, Arcade Fire, Rizzle Kicks Florence Welsh, Lily Allen, Kimberly Walsh to name but a few.

I was really excited and yet terrified to put my name down as I had lost my voice after daddy had died and hadn't really sung again until I was in actor training. Each time I sang, all I could hear in my head was my voice quivering, yet I was so determined to get over this. One of my main career goals was to work in Musical Theatre on the West End and so I had to push through.

I chose a song that would show my acting ability 'I Dreamed a Dream' secretly hoping this may help my dream become a reality.

Mary Hammond worked with me for forty five minutes out of the three hour workshop directing and redirecting me and afterwards advised me to apply for her course at The Royal Academy of Music. I was so thrilled to hear her say that and yet once again that major concern of not being sufficiently talented was in the forefront of my mind. It was like Mary could read my thoughts. She could sense my hesitation and her instincts encouraged her to say those magic words that I so needed to hear.

"You are good enough Pauline! Apply for my course"

Well from that moment I had the fire in my belly with no doubt whatsoever that I would sing again. I now focused on arranging the best singing teacher in Glasgow to work on my voice so that I could gain a place on Mary Hammonds Musical Theatre Course at The Royal Academy of Music.

I did it! I got into the Royal Academy, one of the most prestigious Music Training facilities in the world. I was ecstatic!

I was in RAM Class of 1998 and on the first day I felt like I was walking on air. When walking into the room with all the other newbies I was to meet, I could sense this untouchable feeling in the air. That was talent! I could touch this unbelievable tangible feeling of talent. The energy was so vibrant. Everyone was so excited to be there and yet you could feel the anxious undertones. Suddenly each and every one of us were now the wee fish in this extremely big pond and we were all at the top of our game, so passionate about why we were there and of course, ambitious!

We didn't have time to think that first week, getting to know one another, developing friendships, settling in, as well as understanding the course and the amount of work that was ahead of us.

That's when Imposter Syndrome set in. I began thinking that I definitely wasn't enough in comparison to everyone there.

"All these super talented people around me are going to find out I am shit. Mary Hammond is going to realise and decide that she has made a mistake"

I was coping with these kinds of thoughts all the way through my training. It didn't help that we were working very long hours and I always suffered from sleep issues which went hand in hand with 'the clouds' and training this intensely required you to eat well, which I did, sleep well, which I certainly did not and the lack of sleep always made everything seem much more dramatic in my head.

At the end of the first week we were all extremely exhausted and itching to go out and have a few drinks. A few may be pushing it a bit, a few tons of vodka that is and the next morning I could hardly speak, never mind try to sing. I spent the weekend in silence watching "Sunset Beach" whilst my new friends were still out partying. That is when I discovered that I should never drink vodka. It was like a paint stripper when it came to my voice. From that day I only drank on the holidays so that my voice was able to recuperate. I also stuck to wine consumption from then on. 'Little Old Wine Drinker Me!'

I won the two competitions that were part of the course the H.L. Hammond Prize for Performing Poetry & Prose. This was a prize that Mary Hammond put forward in honour of her father who had recently passed. This competition was judged by British Actor Alun Armstrong known for 'A Bridge

Too Far' alongside Robert Redford, 'New Tricks' as well as nine years spent at The Royal Shakespeare Company. He was also in musicals playing roles such as Thenardier in Les Miserables and the title role in Sweeny Todd.

Performing for Alun Armstrong was so exciting and yet nerve wrecking at the same time. He had after all worked with the amazing Robert Redford. When Alun introduced himself on The Royal Academy of Music's stage he told us how he got into musicals and how nervous he had been when he was first asked to perform in his first West End Musical. He was on location filming a movie with Robert Redford and when they were not on set he would often stay on Robert Redford's sofa. You have to remember this was in the 1970's.

Alun tells us of the story of how he told Robert that he had been asked to do this West End Musical and that he was going to turn it down as he believed he couldn't sing and that he wouldn't be very good. Robert was encouraging him saying that all he needed was to get some training to gain confidence in his own voice. Suddenly Alun heard a woman in the apartment above making these strange sounds and how dreadful they sounded to him.

Alun proceeded to ask Robert if he had to listen to this woman regularly practice what Robert called 'singing'. Robert Redford thought this was hilarious and said that he would invite her down for dinner and he looked forward to Alun telling her what he thought of her singing to her in person.

Later that evening the lady from upstairs came down for dinner and some wine and Robert was teasing Alun to tell the singer what he thought of her rehearsal that he had witnessed through the walls earlier.

Alun was extremely embarrassed and the singer said "You can be honest"

When Alun plucked up the courage and told her that the sounds she was making were dreadful, she smiled and said

"Darling, you have to sound awful to sound great. That was me working through my vocal exercises. You don't think I go on stage and it just comes out do you? You have to sing a song into your voice"

I was waiting with baited breath to hear who it was and of course I was hoping it was my idol. It was the wonderfully talented, Iconic Performer ...

Barbra Streisand

I use this story all the time today to encourage my students that vocal training is not always about sounding pretty. There are also pretty ugly sounds that make a truly wonderful singer.

The second prize that I won at the Royal Academy of Music was The David White Prize for Acting through Song. (David White successes as a West End Musical Director include shows such as Les Miserable and Phantom of the Opera). These prizes came with financial rewards (which believe me, I needed) and my lack of Self Confidence meant I didn't even hear my name being called out as the winner. Claire Marlowe had to dig me on the arm to tell me as she was overjoyed. She knew this could potentially help me feel better about myself. Never before had a student won both of the prizes before me and has never again since.

I am so very proud of this achievement however I couldn't have done it without the amazing tutors I worked with on a daily basis at the RAM.

Singing Teacher Anne James, Voice Coach Annemarie Speed, Acting Coach & Theatre Director Karen Rabinowitz, and West End Musical Directors including Robert Scott, Christopher Hill and the legendary Musical Hall Extraordinaire George Hall. The calibre of teaching was top class, the best around and we were ever so lucky.

When I was invited to a celebration of Mary Hammond in The Theatre Royal Drury Lane I had no hesitation. I just had to be there. The current Royal Academy students performed as well as well as renowned West End performers and as Chris Martin from ColdPlay was also one of Mary's singing students even to this day when he spoke of Mary he had the whole theatre in an uproar of laughter and a standing ovation for her because we all recognised all he had said about her. He also performed his hit 'Fix You' for her as she had worked with him on it, long before it became a huge hit worldwide.

This evening was a huge revelation for me. I was sitting watching these RAM students with bated breath as they were so very talented and then realised I used to be one of them. Wow! That used to be me!

Catching up with all our teachers again was amazing and I couldn't believe how fast the years had passed by and really did feel like I had missed so much of my life.

I can't talk about the RAM without mentioning my amazing friends Claire Marlowe, Lauren Lebowitz Feldman and Myleene Klass. We were all such great friends and their support during and after college means so much to me. We had so much fun together and they would laugh at my rehearsal process as I was obsessive about it. I believed I had to work harder than everyone else, so I did.

They appreciated my personality and Myleene would often accompany me on piano helping me go through songs musically when I needed to. I just had to ask.

They were so generous with their time and they were essential to me during this time and to this day my appreciation and love for them is as strong today as it was then. I send my love and gratitude to all mentioned in this chapter Mary Hammond, other RAM Tutors and friends alike as they made this a very special unforgettable time in my life.

Teaching with Myleene Klass at Performers Inc

In London with Claire & Philip & Mary Hammond

St Johns Wood flatmates Claire Marlowe & Lauren Lebowitz

CHAPTER 16 - THE MECHANIC & I

Although 'The Mechanic' and I were different in many ways we did hit it off at a Birthday Party in1999 when we got together.

At the beginning everything between us seemed so compatible. Life was exciting and we had so much fun together.

By this stage I had gotten my big break in London's West End at The Royal National Theatre – the crème de la crème of theatre. So life seemed like it really was looking up. I was working with one of my Musical Theatre Idols 'Julia McKenzie. I grew up watching her on The Royal Variety Performance performing many Stephen Sondheim hits. She is best known for her role in 'Fresh Fields' and Agatha Christie's 'Marple'. Julia was the director of Honk! The Ugly Duckling by George Stiles & Anthony Drew who later went on to write other successful musicals including 'Betty Blue Eyes', 'Identical', Wind in the Willows as well as re-working the stage version of 'Mary Poppins'

George and Anthony, such a talented team worked very closely with Julia and the cast of 'Honk! The Ugly Duckling' on the Olivier Stage at The Royal National Theatre and that is when we won the Olivier Award for Honk! An extremely proud moment!

I was only in rehearsal a few days when Julia told me she had recommended me to Trevor Nunn for a Shakespeare production also at The National.

That was only THE Trevor Nunn, not only the National Theatre's Artistic Director he had also created in direction the masterpiece 'Les Miserable', 'Miss Saigon' and 'Cats' and here I was being recommended to him for 'The Merchant of Venice'.

These were times in which my dreams were made of a successful career … tick, half decent man … tick. Yet I couldn't shake off the clouds, the anxiety, the feeling, the doubt, the fear and the torture in my head.

My career was flying high and I did have a meeting with Trevor Nunn and I had to perform a piece of Shakespeare for him as one role was acting, then I had to learn a song in front of him and perform it as the second role was of a cabaret singer, also in the Shakespeare play. If you know Trevor Nunn's work, he always does the unexpected.

I was so nervous I can't even explain how much I needed my stomach muscles to work to enable me to sing the song without my voice quivering, but also my 'pelvic floors' because when I got to the high notes. I suddenly felt the hot steam rising up from my trousers and with it the realisation that I was actually pissing myself, I had to do my best acting ever, if I wanted to get these parts and continue working at the National Theatre after Honk. It is safe to say I got the part! Tick ... tick … tick.

Trevor Nunn rated me as a Performer.

The Mechanic loved going to the opening nights at the National.

By now I was working in Rep meaning I was in 3 shows that were running, all on the Olivier stage simultaneously. I was rehearsing Shakespeare as I got to the end of the Honk run and then began rehearsing 'The Villain's Opera' by Nick Deer, a modern version of 'The Beggar's Opera' when 'The Merchant of Venice' opened.

I was spending fourteen hour days at the National and catching forty winks where I could as exhaustion was setting in. You can imagine how I needed to get away from performing when I got home. Needing relaxation and silence was usually what I craved.

This was not what I got however, as I would normally be subjected to 'The Mechanic's amateur performances at family parties, where he would either dress up as a woman (he even had ladies shoes in his size), seemly all his rugby mates dressed up for the craic) or perform anything that would pull attention to him like putting a condom over his head. Exhausting!

All I needed was peace!

He wasn't jealous like 'The Jealous & Possessive', one in fact when I told him I needed to go to a lap dancing club to research one of the parts I was playing in 'The Villains Opera' he was telling me there was a great club near his work called For Your Eyes Only'. In hindsight I wonder if that is where he was all those times he said he was working or visiting his mother?

Anyway I did arrange a meeting with the Dance Co-Ordinator at 'For Your Eyes Only'

Do you ever notice how unglamourous clubs are when you see them in daylight compared to the atmosphere that is created at night with fabulous lighting? This club was dingy. When I walked in it was just really dark in every way, from the décor to the atmosphere and the carpets colour, probably created by the many drinks and other fluids that had covered the floor, as I walked on it, each foot stuck to the ground, squelsh, squelsh, squelsh.

I have mentioned dreams that have come true however I also have had many premonitions before and that sixth sense was warning me once again. I was now getting a really scared feeling in the pit of my stomach. I needed the research so I continued to the meeting with the Dance Co-Ordinator who asked me 'why I wanted to be a pole/lap dancer?

Being an actor, this was obviously great practice, in improvisation. If I could convince this woman I really wanted the job I would already be in character. She said I was 'perfect for the job'. I was thrilled to bits and truthfully I thought if I could do this for research maybe I could actually do this as a job when I am out of performing work. It wouldn't affect auditions because of the working hours. Let's face it dancing topless in a G-string which was really no big deal to me. She told me she wanted me to come back and dance the following night … a dance trial … Naked!

I could feel the sweat rolling down my armpits, but I had to stay in character so I could be introduced to the other girls who were sitting in a booth talking, after all this was also part of my investigation. I also needed to convince them I was genuinely there to be as good as they were at this job in hand.

They cleared up questions that I had, as asking questions helped me to get to hear how they talked, their attitude and mannerisms and the type of things they said. Boy those girls were very clear as you can imagine, 100% financially motivated and not really liking that a new girl was about to join them which could in turn affect their income. Yes it was all about the money and manipulating men into spending their money by cash, cheque, credit card or visa which was actually a line in one of the songs in the show.

I knew I had the job by the time I left. The dance coordinator needed to see that I could dance, which of course I could.

The tension in my body relaxed when I walked out the door I gave a sigh of relief and finally the heavy atmosphere I felt in the club had dissipated. There was no way that I would be going back to that place ever again. To me, really bad things happen in that lap dancing club; I felt chills in my blood! I was only home about an hour when the BBC News reported that a dancer in 'For Your Eyes Only' had just been murdered outside the club. I couldn't move …… One of those girls was now dead, killed by a punter, probably minutes after I had left. You see? When I get a feeling something is wrong … it usually is!

'The Villain's Opera' was doing really well and 'The Mechanic' had come to see it the night of my Birthday and I was at the bar chatting to actor Sue Johnson from' The Royal Family' and Coronation Street's Helen Worth.

Sue was in a play in the Cottesloe Theatre also at The National. I had just come off stage and was getting a drink to begin my celebrations. 'The Mechanic' had been chatting to someone else when Sue Johnston had wished me a 'Happy Birthday' when 'The Mechanic suddenly turned. He then butt in by saying

"It's my Birthday next month!"

"Who are you?" Sue said

I was gutted, here I was chatting to one of the most successful British Actors and she was greeting me on my special day and here he was, trying once again to pull the focus to him.

He said "Pauline's boyfriend?"

"Well as Pauline's boyfriend could you not let her enjoy her Birthday instead of trying to steal her thunder?"

Oh my, she had certainly put him in his place. He didn't know where to look or what to say, which was unusual for him.

Oh Sue Johnston, you really did make me laugh "thank you for that" I said as an aside as only us actors can do so well.

After working on three shows at The Royal National Theatre 'The Mechanic' and I were getting pretty serious. He decided I needed a little break after working such long hours, so I was delighted when he surprised me with a holiday to Cuba!

Wow, sun, sea, sand and even a chance to visit the Hotel International where Al Capone and other Mafia members frequented back in the 1950's and a tropical paradise.

He did wine and dine me and treated me really well and after Cuba he asked me to marry him. I was in love with him and I was already living with him. In the back of my mind, was the decision that I had made, many years ago, "that I would not get married until after I was thirty five"? I believed I would be at the pinnacle of my career by then. I wasn't ready to make that kind of commitment. I was happy with the way things were. So I said 'no'. I tried to explain that I loved him and would marry him one day, but not yet. I could see he was hurt. I don't think he had ever been rejected.

I felt so bad after this and so the nightmares began. I was dreaming that 'The Mechanic' died of a heart attack and he thought I didn't love him. This was paralleling my daddy's death and not being able to say goodbye to him. Now 'The Mechanic' was dead, not knowing I loved him. I woke up in a cold sweat three nights in a row and then I agreed to marry. From then we arranged a wedding six months later.

Not long after agreeing to get married the clouds darkened and I was finally diagnosed with 'Depression'. This was the first time I had heard this word. There was an actual condition to explain what had now been happening to me for nearly fifteen years.

Having a wedding to organise gave me something to think about other than the depression. I was getting used to the medication and now seeing a Counsellor (which didn't seem to help much) I thought the point of counselling was for them to help me work out why I had been feeling this way for most of my life and even though good things were happening I still felt the same.

I felt like I was going on a hamster wheel unable to get off and thought that if she could see clearly where I was going wrong and why I seemed to be going into the depths of despair, at least it would be a start.

The Counsellor just kept telling me, she was there to listen and that I was doing this to myself. So I really was now on a rollercoaster, wasn't the whole point of talk therapy, to help? Instead I was going deeper and deeper into the abyss.

On the eve of our wedding, I began the obsessive prayer that I wouldn't feel depressed on my wedding day. Surely I deserved that? Thankfully the wedding went without a hitch, my mood was elevated and I did enjoy it.

Everything had changed, in his head anyway!

'The Mechanic' and I would usually share the domestic chores such as the cooking, cleaning and laundry, now he said "it was my job "

Was he having a laugh? I was a successful actor and although I hadn't worked for a few months as the depression had come to a head, he knew that I was no housewife.

I went further into depression after this. My new husband who had wined and dined me, made me feel safe, loved and married him was now never at home, always working or at his mothers'. He changed his clothes so often, I couldn't keep up with the laundry, and the washing basket was always overflowing. I had gotten to the point that I was on my own most of the time and I just couldn't cope.

I remember sitting on the chair staring out of the back window and rocking back and forth and then being up in the night as I couldn't sleep for weeks. I spoke to our Deirdre one night about how bad it had become. She encouraged me to go home. She was going to book a flight for me as she was now so worried. When I told 'The Mechanic' this, he was furious.

He said "If you go home, don't come back. We are married now and we should be sorting this together"

But he was never there! I had a panic attack that night

because I now felt trapped.

The dark heavy clouds, the depression, the suicidal thoughts were coming to a head. I now felt I had no way out other than killing myself. As I hadn't slept in weeks of course everything was now exaggerated. I began planning the suicide options. Ways to do the deed and make sure I did it right.

1. Driving over the motorway onto another motorway full of cars. I decided immediately that wasn't fair. What about the innocent people on the road?
2. Driving into the Thames. I knew this was definitely the illness at this point as one of my worst fears is crashing the car into deep water. So there was no way I was in my right mind.
3. All I wanted now was all this to stop! The thoughts, the feelings … life. Mainly I just wanted a break from my own tortured head, sleep would be good, but I knew one tablet wouldn't do it. That's when my head said "Take the whole bottle"

Something shook me out of this. Well what about my poor mummy hearing that I had died of an overdose and not knowing anything was wrong. I had been continually acting that all was good.

I was told afterwards that me thinking of my mother shows that I wasn't as far gone as I thought. Maybe my daddy was looking over at me. I knew at this stage, I was at rock bottom.

So I picked up the phone and called the hospital and told them what I was going to do. I was already an outpatient at Wexham Park Hospital. The girl on the other end of the phone continued talking to me, asking me all the information she needed to get someone to me first, so that I was not alone and then take me to the hospital.

When the Psychiatrist looked at my face he said "You really aren't well are you?"

As I heard him ask this question I nearly fell off the chair in relief. "I would like you to come into the hospital for a rest from life while we look at your medication. Would you like that?"

"Thank God" I said.

'The Mechanic' later told him no wife of his was going into a psychiatric unit.

I spoke my truth finally! For years I knew that this day would come as there had always been something wrong. I knew that one day it would come to an end through death or hospital, so I told 'The Mechanic' in no uncertain terms, that I was staying in hospital. He walked out!

When he came back the next day he told me that he could keep me in the psych ward, as I was his wife and he could sign me in, however I knew I was not sectioned, I was a voluntary patient and knew that was not true but I was still scared … the man I had recently married was that angry with me he wanted me sectioned and was threatening it too. That was the day I really began doubting if I had made the correct decision in marrying him. A frightening prospect, although it was true.

I now know my marriage ended that day only three months in, but it wasn't over yet, I still had a lot of heartache to go through first.

Pauline Carville

On stage at The National

At The National rehearsing for the Olivier Award Winning production of Honk

Cuba 2001

Chapter 17 - Ward 10 Psychiatric Voluntary Hospital Admissions

Most would think going into ward 10 would be a horrendous experience, but for me, it was a relief. Finally someone was listening and most important, really hearing what I needed.

The Psychiatrist had asked me if I wanted to go into hospital for a rest, whilst they worked on my medication. I could have hugged him. I was going to get the help I needed.

He also had put my mind at ease because all those thoughts that were going through my head, I sometimes thought I was hearing voices which had made me terribly worried that something really severe was going on like Schizophrenia but after asking me a few questions he confirmed that it really was my thoughts and subconscious and then gave me the diagnosis of Double Anxiety Depression with a Chronic Low Mood Syndrome. And that he could help me!

I also realised very quickly that although I was ill, I was nowhere near the extent of illness of the other inpatients most of whom were on twenty four hour watch or indeed sectioned, meaning legally they could not leave without a Court Order.

I was advised not to speak of my symptoms to other patients, as it was so easy to start to self-diagnose as there is always a crossover in mental health diagnosis. Hearing from someone else, having similar symptoms, you can understand could send me over the edge.

I was reassured from day one that I would be released swiftly, as hospitals can exaggerate a mental health condition, if I was to be in, for too long. It was a matter of getting enough rest and prescribing the correct medication.

I stayed in hospital for a week in observation as they decided which medication would help get me through this. I was told that this was only the beginning of the recovery stage that could take over a year to really feel myself again.

I was never told though that having waited so long to get the help, over fifteen years to be exact, that it could take as many years after that to really get on top of this condition.

DIARY ENTRY: 2ND APRIL 2001

Today I woke up and instantly started crying. I am just feeling so low at the minute. My heart feels like it is beating out of my chest and I can't seem to be able to get a breath.

All day at college I kept hiding in the toilets talking to my thoughts asking them to stop, of course if anyone saw me I can imagine what they would think?

I feel completely mad and my head is spinning. I keep hearing the voice in my head saying how no one likes me, that I am no good at anything and it would be better for everyone if I wasn't here.

I just want the voice to stop!

I can't cope with all of this, at the same time trying to act like everything is ok.

Oh God my head is away. Please make it stop. Please.

CHAPTER 18 - NEW YORK PSYCHIC

After I had the breakdown and was released from hospital 'The Mechanic' and I moved into a new house.

It was a detached Victorian and it was so grand, sitting on a hill in High Wycombe. You could say it was my dream home until we moved in and then it was cold and empty and I felt like I was rattling around in it on my own most of the time.

By this stage 'The Mechanic' made every excuse in the book to come home late. He was working late and his most popular one was that he was visiting his mother.

I felt so alone. Even when he did come home, he didn't want to be in my company so this was the classic living with someone and feeling lonelier than I would have been, had I actually been on my own.

I was meant to be resting and rehabilitating with the support of my husband and yet he wasn't a bit interested in me and I sensed that he didn't want me there. I was now damaged goods.

After two weeks in the new house I got up one morning and scaffolding was being erected around the house and when I investigated I was informed that the roof was being worked on. Well I remembered 'The Mechanic' had always said that if you buy a house where the roof needs to be improved, do it immediately, as you can then flip it for a higher price. Well seeing the builders working on the roof made me realise that he was definitely up to something. What? I didn't know.

Later that day he was not answering any of my questions, in fact he wasn't communicating with me at all which drove me insane. I was struggling after leaving the hospital and so desperate to feel better and really needing him to support and help me and yet he seemed further away than ever.

He then suggested that I needed a break after everything I had been through and I thought great, he wanted us to go on a holiday and spend time together.

Oh no, he was suggesting that I go away on my own to ….. Wait for it ….. New York! "Why don't you visit your friend Lauren, from college?"

I would always want to visit my dear friend Lauren in New York, but this was certainly not the right time. Who wants to go to New York unwell? 'The Mechanic' was very persuasive and said that it would do me the world of good and that maybe I would feel better when I got back.

I had been in New York before, when I won the scholarship to the top Performing Arts School'. Here I was about to go to the city that never sleeps and I had such fabulous memories and now I was going back like this. I knew this could break me!.

You have to understand that just because I had been in hospital; it didn't mean that the clouds had gone. They were worse than ever!

Now I had to deal with new thoughts of

"Who wants to be around me, everyone thinks I am mad, I

think I'm mad, no one will take me seriously now I have been in hospital"

As well as the obsessive praying, the mind circling, the anxiety, the pins and needles in my arms and legs, the heart palpitations which were all more severe, I was now on stronger medication including sleeping pills and I felt like I was not on the planet.

I also hadn't worked at all this year so it wasn't as if I had plenty of money ready to book a holiday to New York. That is when 'The Mechanic' handed me a cheque and said "This will help you, enjoy yourself".

Well I thought maybe there was enough for the flight and hotels until I looked down and noticed all the 0's.

The cheque was made out to me for £30,000.

In fact he couldn't wait to drop me off at the airport.

I stayed with Lauren for a few days. I was working so hard to act like I was ok because I didn't want her to think she needed to look after me. Looking back now someone should have been, well my husband, but sure he was the one who pushed me to go.

So here I was in the Big Apple and having been here before in happier times I felt so lonely and isolated. I walked around the city like a zombie. I felt like I was having an outer body experience, I could literally see myself walking down the street and every sound was heightened in my head, the car engines, car horns, the walk way beeps, the chatter, the footsteps, so many footsteps, the hotdog vendor trying to get you to buy a dirty big hot dog and this didn't include the loud thoughts in my head.

I am now completely isolated, alone and although Lauren was there also, she was working most of the time, so here I was not only alone, I mean, I was alone in New York, still extremely ill!

Day 4 of my trip to New York I was walking down Madison Avenue completely spaced out and wondering what the hell I was doing there. Tears were streaming down my face and I was walking so slowly especially in comparison to all the speedy footsteps around me. I was amongst crowds of people and I felt completely lost. Not lost in geography, lost in myself.

I got to the point where I was just standing looking around myself not knowing where I was, what I was doing and why I was there, when a lovely woman stopped and asked me if I was ok?

I was in the middle of NYC and someone was taking the time to see if I was alright.

Of course I wasn't ok and was too ill to realise that I was in the middle of a City where I should be very careful of whom I was speaking to. I burst into tears and she invited me to go to her shop for a cup of coffee. Yes I know, what was I thinking? But, that is the point, I wasn't thinking at all! I wasn't capable of thinking. My brain was still going round and round and clearly 'The Mechanic thought, I had been released from hospital just over three weeks now, so obviously I was much better and capable of going it alone in NYC.

So I went back to her shop, which had a table and two chairs in the window which is where I sat while she went to make me a drink.

I sat thinking what kind of shop is this?

 I could also hear a male voice and a little girl's voice and I heard the woman I had met on the street speak in a language that I didn't recognise and then she hushed them, on her way back, as she brought me a cup of coffee.

She sat down at the other side of the table and explained that she was a Clairvoyant and that when she saw me on Madison Avenue, she could see that there was a negative aura around me and realised I was not in a good way.

She tells me that as a child there had been a spell put on me and that I would never be happy until the spell was lifted. Well as if things weren't already bad enough, I had been sacrificed in some way as a child, along with my family and that unless the evil spell was lifted I would never be able to move on.

I was suicidal, even now, even though I had been in hospital, even though I was now medicated, it takes time for medications to go through your system and begin working. It obviously wasn't yet. I started to hyperventilate at the very thought of what she said and her choice of words …. Evil … freaked me out.

 Of course, she was there to calm me down and reassure me that everything was going to be ok because she could help me. I was so relieved, as relieved as any anxiety riddled person can be and she began her ritual.

I was so desperate to feel better I would have done anything! Her ritual that day cost me $150. I would have paid $1500 to get help to feel myself again and that is what she was counting on.

I saw her every day for ten days after this. Day two cost $500, day three $1000 dollars, day four $1500 and you know how the story goes. By day ten my head was fried because I was spending all this money and nothing was easing and in fact I felt like the anxiety was multiplying and I was getting madder each day that passed. By day ten I had spent £10,000.

This is what happens when you hand a woman who has literally just come out of hospital a week after a mental breakdown, hand them £30,000 and send them off to New York, to get rid of them.

Needless to say there was no spell!

You are probably wondering why I didn't speak to Lauren who would have stopped me?

I know I should have. I didn't want her to think that I was still unwell. I am sure she could see that I hadn't fully recovered. Although maybe not?

The Psychiatrist had said that I was such a good actress that most people wouldn't have been able to see how serious things were. I also felt that Lauren would probably have thought I was stupid and you know what, she would be right.

Truthfully I can hear her responding to reading this now all these years later and I can hear her say in her New York accent

"Oh my God Pauline, I never would have thought you were stupid. I would have helped you"

But I didn't give her the chance!

I left New York on day eleven. I had paid for an apartment for a month, but now I was running for my life away from this Clairvoyant as I began getting extremely paranoid thinking that she had control over my mind now and that she would have kept me going to see her until I was broke and unable to get myself home and then I catastrophize so much that I was going to end up living on the streets in New York City. Instead I ran so petrified, home.

I was now traumatised and abused. She was still trying to get money out of me even when I got home. I was ever so vulnerable and I was going to end up in hospital again if I didn't tell someone, so I did the day I arrived back in London.

I realised that this so called clairvoyant was a fraudster when I confided in clearly now my ex's sister and she explained that I had been taken advantage of and advised me to send a text to this New York Con Artist saying that you know her game and that I was going to report her to the NYPD. I didn't hear from her after that.

I begged my Ex's sister not to tell him as I knew he would be furious, however she reassured me that he would understand I wasn't well. I knew he wouldn't. I also knew the relationship was well and truly over for him. He didn't care because if he had felt anything for me he never would have insisted I go in the first place. Besides, who hands someone who is not mentally well that amount of money unless you want out?

When I returned from New York 'The Mechanic' finally dropped the bomb ... He wanted us to separate! He could have saved me the trouble and told me this earlier instead of the latter.

I knew in my heart something was going on. I started to put it all together … the constant changing of clothes, the excuses for coming home late from work, sending his sick vulnerable wife to New York and now a separation. My body shook from inside. I didn't know how I was going to manage. I had gone from a very independent girl to a nervous shadow of myself.

When I moved out, I was not only lonely in this depression, I was alone. My whole support network in London was his family particularly his sister and her husband and their daughter and I know this was so difficult for them. They did support me in so many ways and I really appreciate that. I will always love them! I was now not only recovering from a full mental breakdown, I was now also heartbroken.

My future plans with my new husband were now up in smoke! I begged him to come back to me. I needed to try and fix this, our marriage.

A few weeks later he arranged to take me out for lunch. He got my hopes up. I thought he had been missing me, instead in the middle of a packed restaurant he told me he had been having an affair and although he loved me, he loved her too and felt that she needed him more than I did. I didn't think things could get any worse and here I was. What happened to "For better or worse, in sickness and in health?"

I am not blaming 'The Mechanic' on the depression, however he did add to it. Telling me that "Keen to steal other people's husbands" (that's what I called the other woman) looked after her nails and didn't wear red lipstick and compared me to her, who was not only at our wedding I now realised she was on

157

the other side of him in our wedding photographs. Now he was comparing me to her? What kind of person would do that to someone who wasn't long out of hospital?

Unfortunately my life had now become similar to that of the character in the monologue I mentioned earlier.

"What happened to me? I was young and sexy and you wanted me, now I'm just a nervous wreck. What have I done, where have I gone wrong?"

'The Woman Who Cooked Her Husband'
By Debbie Issit

I was so devastated. My heart was well and truly broken. It was time to go home to Belfast. Back home to family for support and healing.

I Don't Like Being A Woman - My Version #2

I don't like being a woman, I really don't like it!

I don't want to live in a detached house with 2:4 children

With a white picket fence

I want to have Botox, to get the fat sucked out of my chin and anywhere else I can get it sucked out of.

I don't want to do 9 – 5 in an office, I know I can type, but who says I want to type

I just want to be me, I know I don't know what that is yet, but I know what it isn't.

I know I don't always make the right decisions but do you, I mean are all your decisions right?

All I ever wanted was to be an actor. Then I am in the middle of a great career and all my past bites me in the ass. I spent so much time learning how to control my emotions and then bam I am out of control.

So no, I am not sorry for my mistakes, they are my mistakes, because this is my life and I am going to start living it the way I want to live it because for 15 long bloody years I have invested my emotions into other people's lives because I was so afraid to be in my own. .

I want to embrace who I am and if that is me being a little masculine and not lifting the clothes off the floor or doing the dishes as soon as I have eaten then so be it!

I am going to start letting my hair down. Oh and that red lipstick? I'll be wearing it from now on.

By Pauline Carville
Inspired by Monologue in Play
The Woman Who Cooked Her Husband
By Debbie Issit

CHAPTER 19 - THE NARCISSIST WHO NEARLY KILLED ME

When I arrived home from London my focus was my health and I arranged all the things I needed to start my journey to getting well. I had to take another year off to make this happen. Of course it was a very confusing time for me. What was I going to be doing for work here? I had trained as an Actor/Singer and I knew there wasn't a lot of work here in that area, also I felt like if I was to continue performing I would return to London.

Mary Hammond had come to Belfast to do some of her specialised West End Vocal Workshops and asked if I wanted to help her. I did this and that is when Mary suggested that I not only continue teaching Acting as I had done in Red Roofs Theatre School, London, she encouraged me to also teach singing. I now had a goal to work towards.

When I put my business head on, I don't do things by half. Not only did I commence a Singing Lesson Business, I also set up a Performing Arts School 'Performers Inc.' and both became so very successful, at one point I was running four schools around Northern Ireland. This paved the way for me to be able to buy a house and live a nice little lifestyle.

By 2007 in terms of my health I was still suffering from depression daily, not as severe as before as I was now medicated. I had also taken CBT (Cognitive Behavioural Therapy) which had really helped me to manage it. I became more in control of those circling thoughts. I still wasn't entirely myself, but it was a good start.

By now I was beginning to see light at the end of the tunnel.

So when I met 'The Narcissist' I tried to fix all the wrongs in my previous marriage to 'The Mechanic' in this relationship. I went out with 'The Narcissist' for four months and it only lasted that long, as I was so trying to learn from mistakes I had already made, instead of fixing them, I was making an even bigger one.

From the end of the first date I found myself petrified as someone had drugged me when we were out and as he was the only person there, I knew it, in my gut it was him.

I could hardly speak, or walk and my vision was blurred and in slow motion. I even tried calling friends to help me and I could hardly see the buttons on my phone. I told him in my drugged state that I knew that he had done it and he began playing the innocent party and the gentleman and took me home. I had tried to get away from him but he kept reminding me that it was his responsibility to take me home to the door.

The next morning I was blaming myself. I was so embarrassed and wondered if I had imagined it all. 'The Narcissist' called me and said that he was so very worried about me. He totally gaslighted me as if he didn't know what I was talking about and basically said that I had drank too much.

I knew better though as I didn't really drink that much, 3 glasses of wine, as I was on a first date. He persuaded me that it was all in my head and with my previous history I didn't follow my instinct and I continued dating him.

A few weeks into the relationship one of his long term school friends was getting married in Italy and he asked me to join him. At first I said "Yes" and that is where the anxiety began.

I had the fear that something bad was going to happen. This was my intuition working well again and once again I didn't listen.

I went to the Wedding and 'The Narcissist' would be lovely and fun one minute and completely scarily controlling the next. At one point I disagreed with him on something that had happened and he wouldn't let me go to sleep through the night unless I would agree with him.

 Well, me being me, a strong willed woman was definitely not going to do as he said. I went through that torture for five nights straight and eventually agreed that he was right, just so I could sleep. He then tried to persuade me to marry him whilst in Italy, this was only two weeks after we met and now I had been abused for five nights, I think this was his plan to get me so tired...

Thankfully I wasn't that mad, I said 'no way'. I did try to tell his friends what he was doing but he manipulated them as much as he did me.

A few weeks after this, I was due to go on the holiday of a lifetime to The Maldives. He once again manipulated me into letting him come too. I went with him to book it and everything was in place until 6pm the evening before we were due to fly to London.

He called me to say that his friend's dad had died and he was in Donegal. I was in total shock, how was he going to get back to fly to London in the morning. I decided then and there that I would be going on the holiday anyway, nothing was stopping me. He had other plans.

I was getting the final bits of packing done and I knew my

passport had been in a zipped pocket in my handbag and just as I got a little instinctual reminder to check for my passport, so I did.

It was gone! I couldn't move. Where was it? This couldn't be happening to me! Unfortunately it was and immediately I was calling the passport office and crying like a baby to one of my lodgers, who had seen the passport the night before as I had told him everything was ready and showed him the tickets and the passport in my bag.

You know what happened …. I had no passport so I couldn't go on the trip. I had just lost out on my dream trip and £2500 that I had spent on it. I did have a funny feeling that 'The Narcissist' had taken it. It was so strange that he suddenly had to go to Donegal for a funeral.

This all wasn't adding up and then when I started to put the different scenarios together over the last few months including a trip to Donegal where we took a walk along the cliff edge at Gweedore where he was pulling me to the edge and asking me "Do you think you would die if you fell over there?" I was then reminded by his big frightening eyes, in Italy when he kept me awake throughout the week. Now he was controlling whether I was going on this holiday. He clearly had no intentions of going and he wasn't allowing me to go either.

Who was the mad one amongst us? I think it had to be me. I had once again chosen the wrong person. You know what they say "the sign of madness is making the same mistake over and over and expecting a different outcome"

That's it! This was now well and truly over. So I broke up

with him and that is when I had another brush with death, one that I was not in control of!

I was not staying in what I realised to be an abusive, volatile relationship.

We arrived home in a taxi after being out. He trailed me out of the taxi and began beating me. When I was trying to get away from him, he chased me, down the street, and around the back of the houses all while I was trying to run away screaming at the top of my lungs.

 He chased me down the steps to the back door of the house. Each time he caught me he was either pushing his fingers in my eyes, or because I was a singer, he stuck his hand down my throat. He was punching me in the stomach, trailing me by the hair and kicking me down the back steps. He demanded that I open the back door as he had the keys. I tried to avoid opening it as I was hoping the neighbours would be hearing my ordeal.

When we got inside I begged him to let me go to the toilet and I tried to lock the bathroom door but he kicked it in and now he made me go to the toilet and whilst sitting there with my trousers and pants on the floor he watched with eyes that now were so angry, they were red. I saw the devil in him and began to resign myself that this was to be the end of my life.

That's when I began to fight back verbally

"Go on, kill me if that's what you are going to do. My life has been a nightmare anyway; you would be doing me a favour"

He then pulled me by the hair into the bedroom, as he did my bottoms were trailed off, he demanded that I take the rest of my clothes off. He stood there watching me crying in fear, thinking he was going to rape me.

He then pushed me onto the bed and sat his massive body on top of me and then held his hand over my mouth and nose and told me that he was going to kill me.

I fought to breathe which felt like a very long time and as my chest got tighter and tighter I knew in my heart that it was getting close to the end ….. All I could see was my life flashing before me and so far it hadn't been great. I was also seeing my poor mothers face, how would she cope hearing that I had been killed. Then suddenly there was hammering from the front and back door…. Thank God …. It was the Police!

I had endured forty minutes of physical abuse and at one point I was giving up the fight and letting him get on with it. I felt I had had enough of fighting for my life both in depression and now this attack. I did take him to Court; he got 180 hours Community Service and a £200 fine.

I have been fighting for my life ever since, because I deserve a life and a good one at that!

Chapter 20 - What Brought You Back From The Brink?

Let's face it; I had been saved for a reason! Saved from the hands of yet another abusive man and this time I was changing for the best. This really was a wakeup call for me. I really was on my last breath when the Police knocked on the door and saved my life. Thank you!

Someone was there looking over me. Call it what you want. God, the Universe, Higher Power, My Higher Self. Whatever sits well with you! I say this because after my obsessive praying when I was at my worst I avoided using the word GOD.

 I suppose I was angry that I had been through so much and my prayers had not appeared to be answered. My journey through this depression was not over yet. Either way the Universe was a favourite of mine as the whole world was much bigger than I was and that is what I needed.

For me it began with saying I was spiritual. It took me years to realise that maybe what I was praying for was not what the Universe wanted for me. I was asking for what I wanted and not what I needed and that was my error.

My first experience of this was when 'The Mechanic' had told me about the affair. I was starting a temping job the next day and needing the money I had no choice but to get up and go to the office. This is where I met Anita. She was the Receptionist that I would be working with in a very busy corporate office.

I don't know how I kept it together that morning, I just had to act my way through. Anita was showing me the ropes. What an extremely busy reception. The lights flashing when the calls were coming in and I am not exaggerating when I say there were about a hundred and fifty lights and sometimes around fifty lights were flashing at the same time. I was so emotional, I didn't have time to burst into tears, but when there was time, I had no control. Once the madness of the ringing phone lines stopped, I started!

At morning break Anita brought me into the tea room and asked if I was ok? She could clearly see I wasn't. I kept thinking she must think I am completely mad coming to a new job in this state. I told her about the marriage break up after a long struggle after the breakdown, being in hospital, in recovery and now this. How much more could I take?

She listened with such compassion and just said

"Would you mind if I prayed for you?"

"What here?" I said

I thought about how desperate I was, if someone wants to pray for me, let them. So she did. She prayed that I have peace and to be able to get through the day. I must admit a real sense of peace did come over me at that moment. She explained that if I was in agreement that she would arrange her Pastor and his wife to pray over me that evening after work.

Wow! This woman that I had only met a few hours ago really wanted to help me. Yes I do remember the New York Psychic; however I really did feel that Anita was genuine. After work the Pastor, his wife and Anita prayed over me. The first time I had experienced this kind of praying.

Afterward the Pastor explained that God may not want me to get back with my husband, that he had betrayed me and that God doesn't want me to be in pain. "Ask God what he wants for you instead" he said "And then, wait"

A few days later, I had my answer! Going home was playing over and over in my head and I took this as a sign. It was time to go HOME and that's what I did. I went home with faith and a little bit of hope too. I had definitely had some kind of Spiritual experience and that was ok for now.

After 'The Narcissist' nearly killed me, I was introduced to 'The Spiritual Life Coach'; this has been a Godsend. She had this angelic look about her and her presence I can only describe as heavenly. I had Reiki, which is an alternative therapy from Japan where healing is transferred from the therapist's hands through a Universal energy for emotional and physical healing.

She helped me develop a tool kit to calm myself down when I was in a full on anxiety state. She taught me breathing techniques to slow down the panicking and how to meditate.

I began to hand my problems or decisions to a Higher Power each morning which seemed to really work for me. 'The Spiritual Life Coach never used the term "God", ever, that was up to me if and when the time was right.

Over the years 'The Spiritual Life Coach' has become my mentor and friend. She is always there when I need an ear. She is so supportive and understanding and knows my story and what can make me feel out of sorts. She genuinely cares.

It was 'The Spiritual Life Coach' that encouraged me to go and see The Psychotherapist as she felt that there were deep rooted issues that only a Psychotherapist could get to the bottom of.

I have since had many spiritual experiences that are not by chance or definitely of this earth and now I am 100% certain that there is a "God"

Every morning I now get up and go outside to my little covered terrace that I had made so that I could come out rain or shine and hand my decisions up to God. I found that over the years I have learnt that I only want what is right for me and when I give those over to God I don't worry about my decisions.

I asked God to not let me go through another break up and that the next man was the right man. (That's a story for later though). When I was moving back to Belfast, I asked to be guided to the right house where I would feel at peace and want to live long term. I didn't think it was possible, but here I am in a house with the most striking views over Belfast with the country and the Castlereagh hills as my garden. Two major milestones in my life and I feel like I was guided by God, the Universe, a Higher Power or you could even say my Higher Self. All I know is that it works!

I also spoke daily to my Daddy, whom I knew and felt that he was watching over me. I had been speaking to him since he died when I was fourteen. I know that it was he that was there when 'The Narcissist' was attacking me.

Spirituality has also been a journey that has taken time for me to accept and trust over many years and certainly not in an obsessive way like before. I ask for guidance every day and that works for me.

Of course all this was supported by my wee Mummy and my family who are always there for me during the tough times however at the end of the day to be fair on my Mummy and family, they are not experts in mental health, so it was my duty to myself to seek out any means that would help me through these rough times and that's what I did.

I am now really clear on how I live my life if you ask. It is in a Spiritual way. God led.

I really do believe that our relatives that have passed over onto the other side are looking out for us here on earth, as our Guardian Angels, you could say.

So what really brought me back from the brink of suicide all those times?

God did!

Chapter 21 - Friendship & Jealousy: Do They Go Hand In Hand?

I do have to admit that my relationship disasters were not all down to men! I have always been so open and honest, maybe too open. You see I expected everyone to be like me, but they aren't.

I now have a very strong opinion on what I consider to be a good friend!

Friendship is a relationship, just like any other which requires honesty, loyalty and mutual respect. I don't do something to you that I wouldn't want done to me.

I need to know that I can say something to my friend and know that whatever I say will go no further. My best friend's know this about me and this is completely mutual. With really good friends I always feel that it doesn't matter at all how often I see them, it usually feels like nothing has changed. I love that! When I become your friend, you have a friend for life. Unless you do something to break that bond.

I will always give people the benefit of the doubt and also I believe I give people many chances to repair that bond or apologise if it is warranted. Although through life's experience I have learned that if you do something once on me whether it is verbal act on your part and you apologise, I will put it down to a genuine mistake, if you do the same again I may also let it go, however if you repeat something that you know is derogatory to me or hurtful, that will be that! Once something has been done to me repetitively, that is when you have crossed my boundary and I will happily zap you from my life.

I wasn't always like this. I didn't have boundaries in place during my life and have been hurt by a few people that I considered to be my friends. After experiencing being treated badly three to four times, I learnt what my non-negotiables are. If you do something that you know will upset me, then you are being disrespectful and now, thankfully I am really clear on that. I wasn't always. I had to learn the hard way, but isn't that part of life?

To me, a friend must be trustworthy and loyal. I have heard it said that

'When someone needs something from you, they are loyal. Once that person's need is fulfilled by you, their loyalty comes to an end'.

I can say that I have experienced this with about three or four friends in total (if you would call them friends?) . These friends worked with me in some way or another or I involved them in working with me in my business. I say with, rather than for me, as I genuinely believe that anyone that works in my business, they are working with me as well as for me. I suppose what I mean is that we are a team and work together, although there has to be some respect in the sense that I own the business. As long as there is mutual respect there is never a problem. Maybe that is why it is also been said 'Don't mix business with pleasure' this is because it is easy for the boundaries to get blurred. I just don't like it when someone takes advantage of my good nature.

What I have learned through these friendship break ups, is that usually someone being unfriendly, disrespectful or saying untoward words to me, it has been down to one, word, and one word only. JEALOUSY! 'The Green Eyed Monster' is how it is otherwise known.

To tell you the truth I never really understood the concept of someone being jealous, especially jealous of me because of how I felt inside. I mean, who in their right mind would want to be like me, in any way? Maybe it was because I was so good at externally portraying confidence, strength, and happiness to the outside world. I think I can understand it more now, that I am not deep in depression.

So throughout my life I do believe that those people, who upset me, were removed from my life, Spiritually. Why were they removed? They all had some kind of jealousy. I cannot fathom why anyone would have wanted to be like me? Could they not see how miserable I was? Life was tragic and I had to act that everything was ok, all the time. However as I discovered through time, there was always something that I had, that they wanted. That is how jealousy works!

I believe that God or the Universe removes those who are not serving a purpose in our life or affecting our energy, confidence and positivity. I find that when we are vulnerable and unwell, some people do take advantage and those who do that are usually the ones that are closest to you and you consider them to be a great friend that is when it hurts the most, when you realise.

I didn't know what I had to offer or be jealous of. So those who wronged me wanted something I didn't even know I possessed.

Through therapy, I now wonder if it was my talent, my

personality, my determination, my organisational ability, my ideas and imagination, my business acumen.

I mean were they jealous of my illness?

Somehow I don't think so and yet to me that was my life. The clouds, the darkness took over everything in my life because I was completely crippled with anxiety and depression. Every breath I took was a dark thought, every second, every minute of every day I struggled with the clouds and the manifestation of those clouds physically. So anything that I did in my life training as an actor and a singer I really had to make myself do everything obsessively because by religiously practising something or repeating something in my head over and over helped me to stay in control.

I couldn't understand why someone would be jealous of that?

What I can say is that after these so called friends are no longer in my life, in whichever way this has taken place. I always feel it has been for the better. I have realised that they have been having a negative impact on me and when they are gone there is definitely a positive feeling and that is when I realise something spiritual has taken place. Thank God!

I now realise that you can't do or say anything to me that I haven't done or said to myself. I am my worst critic! I am harder on myself than I will ever be on anyone else. So, if anyone talks about me or trolls me on social media I laugh and think, if I have gotten through Depression, then I can get through anything.

So think again!

Chapter 22 - The Next Relationship Has To Be…

After all the relationship disasters, I decided that "No More Tears (Enough is Enough)" as in the 1979 song performed by Barbra Streisand & Donna Summer. No making the same mistakes over and over again and expecting a different outcome. It was well and truly the time to put boundaries in place, but where do I start?

I remembered seeing a Relationship Counsellor when I first came back from London and she had asked me

"What do you want in a man?"

So I listed off all the usual things

- Confident
- A strong personality
- A great sense of humour
- Generous
- Ambitious
- Trustworthy

I am sure you see where I am going with this! To my utter surprise the Relationship Counsellor said

"That list, is what you want for yourself Pauline"

You could have knocked me over with a feather. Could this actually be true?

She continued: "This list is why your relationships don't work.

You are choosing men who mirror you!

I have to admit, this was a real eye opener. I was in shock and very quickly all those words describing what I thought I wanted in a partner, I could instantly see my relationships flash before me, now seeing so clearly that I had always been going out with a man who was exactly like me.

It was time now to dig deep and think about the qualities that I not only want, but need in a Life partner.

So how would I know what qualities in a person would work with my personality and characteristics? That is when I did some research and found an internet dating site. I had never gone onto one of these sites before however I was really interested when one of these dating websites asked me to fill out a form detailing my personality, my likes, dislikes etc. They then sent back to me based on my answers the type of man I could be looking at.

This was when I made a new list …

- Honest & Trustworthy
- Compassionate
- Empathy
- A good listener
- Understanding
- Probably quieter than me (because I talk so much)
- Confident
- Makes me laugh
- Makes me feel good when I don't
- Smart Dresser

These were just to name a few on my list and then the most

important was to be

- SUPPORTIVE

AND

- LOVE ME FOR ME! For who I am. Warts and all!

After making this list I began taking advice from the "Law of Attraction" book "The Secret". I began decluttering my home. Everything and anything connected to a person, place, situation in my past that was negative, whether it was clothes, furniture, jewellery, make up, even Christmas decorations – anything with a memory of an Ex or the negative past. It was all thrown out!

Finally there was space in my head, my wardrobe and my heart for someone, when the time was right.

Truthfully, I had decided that I was happy on my own. I felt that I preferred being on my own protecting myself, my mind, my heart. What was the point in being with someone if they didn't make me feel good about myself?

I began to enjoy my solitary life. I focused on my work and looking after me and I enjoyed going out at the weekends with my friends. I also started to pray. Yes for the first time in years I was praying and you might be surprised at what I said in that prayer.

Lord

I have now gotten to a place where I feel safe and secure on my own. I truly am happy to live my life alone if that is what is meant for the rest of my days. I am at peace with that. If you do have a plan for me to have a partner, I pray that the next person I put time into, that he is the one. I ask this, because I just cannot go through another breakup. I just can't! Please God, not another breakup. I just can't deal with another broken heart.

Amen

Within months, I met Robin!

Chapter 23 - Meeting Mr Elegant

I had been working as a Performing Arts Lecturer at Belfast Metropolitan College since 2005 as well as running my Performing Arts School, Performers Inc. as well as the singing school. Yes, I liked to keep myself busy. I did also work in the Media Department at the college and that is where one of the tutors who had realised what I did outside of lecturing had mentioned that she believed that I should meet Robin Elliott.

If I am honest, having lived in London for such a long time, the local celebrity scene was really not of interest to me and I didn't really listen to much radio unless in the car. I had heard his name, but had absolutely no idea what he looked like and as he was a Presenter, I really didn't understand why she believed that a meeting with this man was what I needed.

I realised that she was trying to encourage me to not only teach, but to get back to doing what I started out doing .... performing! I was happy at this stage teaching and living in my little bubble focusing on other people and not on myself. So you must realise I never really gave anything this colleague was suggesting much thought.

There were so many opportunities where I could have met Robin and yet none of these happened ... obviously not the right time!

I did one day hear this Robin Elliott on City Beat whilst driving past Forestside shopping centre and did think what a fabulous Presenter he was. Then another day I heard Stuart Robinson announce that one of the broadcasters had released a single. It was Robin Elliott in 2008 singing, well, speaking I should say 'The Ballad of Lucy Jordan'

I spoke aloud to the radio and said

"Who is this eegitt DJ trying to sing?"

I did finally meet Robin in the car park of Belfast Metropolitan College in Castlereagh having worked there since 2005 and that colleague said

"Wow! Finally! Pauline Carville, meet Robin Elliott"

I have to admit I was a little overcome with embarrassment. I couldn't understand why and when she said

"Robin this is the girl I was telling you about"

Robin replied "Let's arrange a meeting next week"

I said "No you're ok, don't worry about it"

I didn't know why I would be having a meeting with him and that was my way of dismissing it, as swiftly as possible. I don't think Robin had ever been turned down for a meeting before and I think that made him notice me even more ... although not my intention. I just wanted to hide how scundered I felt.. (Scundered) Belfast for embarrassed)

A few days later I did need Robin as I was having a panic attack and needed support and my friend wasn't in and I just got the feeling that if Robin was, he would probably be able to help me. He did, he was really great actually and we talked for about 15 minutes and that is where it all began in the corridor of Belfast Met.

Not long after we were together I realised that our first meeting had a magical feeling as if we had been brought together by the Universe. There was a strong spiritual connection. We connected in body, mind and spirit and of course music. (If you want the full story that would be a book in itself).

We married on the 23rd May 2012 in a true show biz style wedding at The Island Arts Centre Theatre. We were both from performing backgrounds and this totally made sense to us. We arranged the wedding together within 6 weeks (who says you need more than that to plan a wedding?) we arrived in a limousine with a few of our friends as we felt like we were married already and this was a legal formality and yet it was so very romantic.

We kept the wedding really simple, having our reception in our friend's restaurant 'Nu Delhi Lounge' and had all our showbiz friends including our dear friend Des Lee and Barry Woods from The Miami Show Band who sang on the day. We partied into the wee small hours.

The wedding has been followed by many, many more adventures including a move to Tenerife, setting up our own Theatre Company and producing shows in Theatres across Belfast including the Grand Opera House and ending up on T.V. together. I guess I will have to keep those stories for another day.

Through Robin I met one of my all time favourite movie

idols, Hollywood Star Maureen O'Hara!

I told her about how my mental health had put an end to my acting career as I had returned home to Belfast to get well. I explained how, at that time I was considering going back to London to get back to what I started and I wasn't sure if I really wanted that now. I explained that being ill had put a lot of things into perspective and I had been there and done it and felt maybe it was time to find another passion. Her response was simply

"You have been through alot and achieved a lot also. My advice is to do only what you love now and you won't go wrong"

I really heard her advice that day and now I really only do what I love. I have realised that our loves and desires change through life and that you go with those changes too.

Although I lived the glamourous theatre lifestyle with fans waiting outside the theatres I performed in, I really never took that too seriously. Maybe that was a touch of the Imposter Syndrome again. "Why would anyone want my autograph?" even though I was in these hugely successful shows.

When I met Robin, His status was that of a Celebrity and therefore recognised everywhere we went. I was proud to be with Robin and as I felt secure in our relationship I was able to enjoy it. Afterall the attention wasn't focused on me. So I could be rather chilled out.

What I did find out quickly is that Robin could be out at an event every night and that was exhausting for me, as Robin was happy having me with him on his arm and I obviously wanted to be there to support him.

After a time it did become a little overwhelming for me as I didn't want or need to be in a false environment, with the showbiz fake smiles and the same chit chat every time. If I wasn't feeling at myself, the last thing I wanted was to be around that acting pretence. I had spent enough time pretending in my life, I didn't have the energy to do that anymore.

I do feel different now. I feel like I have come full circle. I have been working as a Presenter with Robin on The Big Show from time to time and being recognised on the street and I am ok with that. This proves to me how far I have come on my journey to being healthy and mentally well.

What I can say is that my relationship with Robin has made me what I am today. He is my best friend in life and work and he is my soulmate. He has helped me face the depression and my past head on through his patient, understanding manner and ability to listen.

We have so much fun together and Robin knows by my behaviour or my face (as it tells all) if I am "not right" and changes my focus through making me laugh or taking me out for a walk on the beach.

I finally chose the right one!

With Shane Lynch

With Robin on our wedding day

The Carville Family at the elegant wedding

Appearing at the Winter Gardens in Blackpool with Joey Essex &
Robin Elliott

Fun night out. Janet McGregor and Robin Elliott

Chapter 24 - A Tribute To My Wee Mummy

My Mummy became my best friend after I returned home from London. I finally let her in!

She was there for me for every step I took. Even when she watched me make new mistakes, she was always there to help me pick up the pieces.

I only wish now I had realised what an ally she was to me sooner. | Maybe I wouldn't have suffered at the hands of my own secrecy. Trying so hard to protect her, believing she wouldn't be able to cope seeing her youngest daughter in so much pain.

Oh how wrong was I?

My Mummy was the strongest woman I have ever known and I am so grateful that I had her love and support until she passed away on 6th March 2014.

Thankfully she saw me happily married to Robin. She knew that we were really good together. She knew that Robin really loved me and she loved him too!

I understand now that my Mummy too suffered from depression through her life, particularly after my Daddy's sudden death 28 years before.

She always said she had us! Her children to look after! Selfless to the very end!

Thank you!

I love you Mummy!

This poem is for you and Daddy!

GREENORE

Here is Mummy by my side
Down at old Greenore
As we sit quietly looking out to Shore
Deep in thought, the both of us

I see the beauty and why he loved it here
Mummy says "It's beautiful isn't it?
And as I say "Yes" we both give a deep sigh
Of relief

The sun sparkling on the ocean blue
The Cooley Mountains behind, so green
Oh I now can see what you and Mummy seen

Mummy sits so still and quietly
As we both, breathe in this scenery
Her memories just as beautiful and more
As the two us sit quietly
On the shore of old Greenore

Chapter 25 - Child, Or No Child: That Is The Question!

You may have wondered if I ever had children. The answer is no! I was never really that maternal in my younger days!

I suppose to me having a child was a lifetime job, not to be taken lightly!

I was so focused on wanting to be an Actor, I didn't want anything to get in the way of that.

Sounds selfish, doesn't it? Maybe it was at the time, although I remember hearing about one of my Daddy's sisters who was allegedly more interested in going to the local Drama Society, leaving her children to be looked after by her husband, mother, sister or anyone who would have them, so she could go and perform on stage.

I never wanted to be that person! I believed that becoming someone's Mother was an honour, but definitely a choice that you had to make.

My choice was not to have children or at least wait on thinking about having children when my career was where I wanted it to be.

If I am really honest, I just didn't have that desire that some women have. Not like the passion I had for Acting, Singing and Performing. To me if the desire wasn't there then it was not a selfish choice, more like a selfless one!

Why bring a child into the world unless you are 200% there for the wee innocent being? However, later I did wonder if having a baby would be a life changing decision I could make. After all, I had tried everything. I had been a successful Actor in London, although it was cut short. I travelled the world and ran businesses. I had achieved a lot of my career goals. Maybe a baby would be a perfect addition to my life, as long as I was with the right person to co-parent with?

How could I? I had spent most of my life struggling to get through the day, dealing with myself and my own demons. I felt like I could just about manage myself. Would it be fair to bring a child into that? More importantly, would that child grow up as I did with anxiety and depression? I just couldn't take that chance!

So no, I didn't have a child of my own, not because I was selfish or self-centred, but because it was the right thing to do!

I am really good with children and I have worked with children through teaching performing arts and some I have watched grow into adults who went on to follow in my footsteps and become professional actors, singers or both. I can enjoy their energy, talent, innocence and laughter without ever feeling guilty that if I had gone ahead and brought a child into this world and not be able to give them my full attention. Well I believe that would be the biggest mistake anyone can make in this life.

Children really are, our future as the Whitney Houston song says and I am really happy, because I did the right thing and I can be proud of that.

The only concern I did have recently is that I won't ever have my husband and/or children at my death bed as my Mummy had at hers.

Again, not a good reason to have a child!

Now when I think it all through … Child or no Child! There were so many times that I could have conceived over the years with Robin. Do you understand what I am saying? It never happened, not even by "accident" as many say.

Now I wonder whether or not I could even conceive?

You could say that it was just not to be part of my life's journey …

Motherhood!

CHAPTER 26 - THERAPY OUTCOME: HOW DID IT ALL GO HORRIBLY WRONG?

It is very hard to think back to those times, and it even makes me very emotional talking about it right now, because depression is something that you constantly have to work at. There are still days if I am out with Robin at an event and I see people looking well and laughing and appearing really happy, and maybe that particular day I am not feeling very well within myself, maybe I feel fat, or ugly, or I look at what everyone is wearing and I think "Why did I wear this, I clearly have no taste"

I know it sounds crazy because there is no reason even now and because we are photographed together a lot when I look back at the photographs afterwards I go "What was wrong with me, I looked amazing that night" You know, as in, what I believed to be amazing looking for me. It has to be that I thought, I looked well or felt I looked well. It doesn't matter how much Robin would reassure me and say how gorgeous I looked and he does that on a regular basis. It was only afterwards, when I was able to look at the photographs and go Wow!

And that's the thing even when I look back at old photographs from various times in my life, I can see, I remember exactly how I felt in the different scenarios and yet when I look at those now I can see how no one could see what was going on because I really was that good at hiding it. I did look gorgeous, I looked happy, even my demeanour, my physicality, my poise, everything I did in those photographs captured that I was ok.

I had gone through this psychological process on a number of occasions and telling The Psychotherapist my story and explaining every deep thought, all my mistakes, feelings, decisions and disasters, I had already told so many therapists that preceded him.

"You were true to your word. You dug deeper than anyone before"!

The Psychotherapist was asking me to divulge different aspects of my life and had also mentioned that writing a diary or just logging what I was learning as I went through the therapy journey was extremely therapeutic and as anyone desperately wanting help, I was willing to do anything to climb over that wall that I had built.

It's funny, of course I knew exactly the type of questions he would ask and more importantly how he may ask them, to get me to face the intricate details that I had been blocking and hiding not just from the people who truly cared about me, but also from myself!

I had pushed my feelings so far down that I had no idea what had started me on this dark journey – the life I had been living for 30 years.

I understood that I would be asked about major milestones in my life to date including my childhood from age five to eight (they all do) and that was just the start.

By now I was beginning to realise how much I had hidden from myself, even the good memories were sacrificed. I did however explain that I was a happy child as far as I could remember and that is when he pushed me further.

He asked

"Is there anything you can remember that could have become an issue?

I would blankly stare "No"

"What about School?" He said

The light was switched on!

I do remember struggling in Primary four. I had a teacher for years P4 and P5 – 'Mrs A'. I had told her I was really having great difficulty with understanding maths and couldn't see the black board from where I was sitting. I was sure that she would sit me at the front of the classroom to help me and make it easier to see, I had already told mummy and she had made an appointment for me to get my eyes tested. I always felt like 'Mrs A' left me out and even when I would put my hand up to ask a question or say I didn't understand she seemed to ignore me.

Instead of moving me to a desk at the front … She put me to the back of the classroom. She didn't appear to care and from that day on I believed that a negative belief system began. You speak up, you get punished and so I began to tell myself that I clearly wasn't "good enough". (This thought followed me through life and even today I have to work really hard not to let that thought in).

From that moment I had severe nightmares and I walked in my sleep on a daily basis. It got so bad I was opening the front door of our house and lining up the kitchen chairs in the front driveway in military precision, like we did in the class clean up at the end of the day. 'Mrs A' was controlling me in my every waking moment and now she was in my dreams. I guess I was trying to be the good girl to make her like me ... it didn't work!

I didn't remember the sleep walking, until one Sunday morning Mummy and Daddy sat me down in the living room and explained to me what had been happening and that they were going to the school on Monday to get to the bottom of what was going on.

At this stage I didn't understand how they knew what had been taking place in school, until they explained that I had been sleep walking again and that I had in fact told them everything in my sleep.

Mummy did go to the school and of course the principal and teacher pulled ranks and stuck together, this was certainly not the end for my Mother. When the doctor was concerned enough to refer me to a Child Psychiatrist, he said that it had become a psychological issue.

After working with me for six weeks the expert made a report which explained that the issue was coming from a form of bullying by the teacher which was causing the nightmares and the sleep walking.

Now Mummy had evidence to show the principle in the school and from that moment on things in the school changed for me. However, a year later the bullying began again, this time with my younger brother Brendan. He was a nail biter, I think he still is and can you believe it this very teacher stopped my brother from being included in the class in verbal and written communication as well as tying his hands behind his back to stop him from biting his nails?

Unfortunately the seed had now been planted in my head. "I wasn't good enough" and from then on, I struggled with Low Self Esteem and a severe lack of confidence. It was just as well even at this age, around eight, I loved performing and although you might think how could she do that with no confidence? This really was the beginning … I just acted!

I began life imitating art. I remember the Abba song 'Super Trouper' was number one at this very time and I decided that I was going to be a 'Super Trouper' and that's when I painted on a smile and began the 'Performance of my life'. I continued through my teens and early adulthood pretending that I was a very confident person. I thought if I acted ENOUGH … it would come true!

After this, anyone that I thought was an authority figure, someone who could stand in the way of me getting on and achieving my life goals, I repeated the pattern the feelings of fear, rejection, loss and anxiety.

Deep down inside I was so not confident, in many respects, desperate to let out the real me, but I just couldn't! I had somehow lost myself along the way and now really didn't know who Pauline was?

Understanding when my problems really began was essential to my recovery. Me, Pauline, the adult could see clearly that wee girl In that Primary School, at age seven or eight that was left frightened and alone to fend for herself.

I just couldn't believe that between the bullying by that teacher, the rape of Hannah in Belgium and the death of my wee mate Elina. I was so traumatised in such a short space of time that I hid it from myself as I obviously didn't know how to handle it.

I am so grateful to The Psychologist, 'The Spiritual Life Coach' and everyone including my family for helping me to see where this all came from.

You may already have deciphered what was going on behind those brick walls that I had built around me. The truth is it really wasn't just one event. As a child I was already having some issues at the age of eight in school being blanked and ignored by the primary school teacher, which I understand now to be abusive, the vivid nightmares and the sleep walking. I now understand that having a traumatic experience this young can affect your future life.

If this had been the only trauma I may have been able to process this and move on however then the Belgium fiasco happened where my intuition kicked in that something terrible was going to happen and then it did, so this felt like confirmation that if I dream or get a feeling that something terrible is ahead, then major fear set in and so the anxiety began. Then my daddy died and this affected our whole family dynamic, the shock and I blamed myself.

This was all happening up to age fourteen in a seven year cycle. My understanding now is that if one traumatic event happens in a seven year cycle it is difficult enough but to have three in such a short space of time, it was obvious these events were the trigger for anxiety. I also comprehend now that if I had dealt with this through therapy and support it probably wouldn't have lasted this long.

Instead I painted that smile and acted my way through and then continued to make decisions through an unstable mind until I hit rock bottom. Thankfully I did hit the depths of despair otherwise I would still be going through this. The breakdown or breakthrough as I call now, was the beginning of me turning all this around. It took ten years to get through and still I felt that I wasn't truly over it and that is where acceptance comes in.

This was the breakthrough! This expert helped me to see clearly and finally I could begin the process of mending that childhood pain. Everyone blamed my daddy's death and yes at this stage I was also able to grieve properly for my daddy and also begin working through other fears like how I would deal with my mummy passing too.

The Psychotherapist helped me to understand that I was in a very different place now and that I had to realise that it is inevitable that one day my Mummy would die and that you cannot prepare for that.

Not long after this discovery my wee Mummy passed away and when I thought I was going to fall apart I just thought "Mummy doesn't want you to go back into oblivion as I had recently called it instead of 'The Clouds'. She wants you to be strong and remember her the way she was"

That is what I have done ever since, knowing her and Daddy watch over me daily.

As I sit here in The Psychotherapist's room I feel like I have answered all his questions and more importantly I have now finally answered my own.. I knew that I still had a road of true recovery ahead, however for the first time I totally understood how this all began and this really was a revelation!

After years and years of misery and desperation I could now see clearly for the first time. No clouds! I knew I wasn't completely cured. It took over thirty years to get to this point. It may just take as many to really feel completely cured, if that is even possible? You see, I also believe that accepting that I may have to always work on myself to keep anxiety and depression at bay is life changing.

I may one day feel low, or even feel depressed, however I am really clear on this, I will not use the word depression, unless it really is Depression!

The question now in my head is still am I mad?

So I answer it for myself for now. Maybe I am, however I am learning each day about what I don't want and voicing it rather than hiding it and maybe that is a start?

I do have to say that society, including me to date, uses this term "mad" or "depressed" on a daily basis.

"I'm mad because of the decisions I make, he's mad because of the relationships he stays in, she's mad because of what she wears"

When I ask if I am mad? I am talking about being ill, mentally unwell and those feelings and continual thoughts of suicide, deep dark depression where I cannot function.

You also hear way to often "I'm Depressed" when all you mean is that you are having a low day or something someone has said has made you feel low and maybe you have split up from a long term relationship or maybe even lost your job and these situations can make some people feel 'depressed' of course they can.

I would just ask you not to use this word fleetingly because words have power and believe me you really do not ever want to go through what I have. I wouldn't wish it on anyone!

Now there is no point in me asking the pertinent question in my head. Keeping things hidden has clearly not worked for me in the past. So I decided that I have to say it out loud.

I ask myself again "Am I mad?"

Well I did spend so much time acting other people and expressing their emotions through me. Maybe I lost myself along the way? I do think a performer needs to be a bit mad (in the fun sense) to want to play other people in the first place. Don't you think so?

So I finally asked 'The Psychotherapist'.

"Am I mad or what?" Come on, you know his answer, he is a mental health professional. He is not going to say yes is he? A bit like Politicians answer a question with a question.

He says

"What do you think?"

All I have gone through for over thirty years has made me the extremely strong woman that I am today! So in answer to your question

Yes, yes I am!

And you know what?

I LIKE IT!

Age 7

Epilogue

Now I seek peace, peace of mind and spirit. Everything I do now is to achieve this peace.

So no, my Singing and Acting career is not something I want now. I do a little here and there when the notion takes me but it has to feel right. I was such a good Actor and singer because I took emotional risks that put my mental health in jeopardy.

 I believed that being an actor was all there was to me, but it wasn't. I believe to be a truly successful actor you need balance of Body, Mind & Spirit so when someone asks me now about performing whether it is a play or singing in a band I always check in with myself, meditate on it because chasing a dream was the old me.

I now love silence, which is unusual for a singer, singing teacher and vocal coach. That doesn't mean that I don't want to sing or teach, it just means that most of my week after working I enjoy the silence.

The quiet is what I seek in my mind as it can still race and can be extremely loud at times. Certainly I find that when my mind is noisy or circling, it is a sign that I need a break, some me time. I think everyone needs quiet time and yet most of us avoid it.

I have discovered through my own experiences that I have to listen to myself when I need that tranquil space and time otherwise my mind gets so noisy I want to bash it against a wall again. Yes even now!

When I see or hear the signs I listen now. I either go for a walk along the beach, meditate in my own back garden which I have made into a peaceful space or if my head is really noisy I get away for the night somewhere quiet obviously as sometimes a change is as good as a rest. This obviously isn't somewhere with a noisy bar, it is just going back to basics, totally simplifying life for me, is therapy.

So if I learnt anything from that it is not to avoid my overzealous mind, to listen to what it needs. I think as the years have gone on I have learnt more and more about myself and what works for me and listening to myself because deep down I know what is right for me and so do you!

MY MENTAL HEALTH TOOLKIT

Mind Set is an essential part of our daily lives and looking after our mind set is as important as feeding and clothing yourself. Drinking water and looking after our physical bodies. Our cars need fuel to work, so do we!

Everyday behaviours become a habit if you do them enough and I have found that looking after your mental health is about changing your daily behaviour and changing your daily beliefs.

You see, the more you repeat something, the better you get and then daily practice will change your belief system. We all have core beliefs that don't always benefit us and we can change them, if we really want to.

This is my daily routine and I hope it helps you!

1. Thank the Universe for the great sleep that I have just had and then I say the Serenity Prayer. This is a prayer that they use in Alcoholics Anonymous to help them to stop drinking. I am not an alcoholic however it works as I am asking for 'the acceptance of things I cannot change, the courage to change what I can and the wisdom to know the difference' and this is a great positive start to the morning.

I also surrender my will, my problems, my decisions (whatever I may get anxious about) to the Universe, the sky if you like, just as long as it is not in my/your head

Each morning, I go out to an outdoor covered terrace that I had made so that I can do this. You can create this anywhere, even a little corner in your bedroom.

I cannot express enough how this works for me. This was something I learned from 'The Spiritual Life Coach' and I don't think it even matters if you are spiritual or not. Think of handing this to your Higher Self if that works for you, just so it is not inside your mind.

2. Mindfulness!

Keeping your mind on exactly what you are doing at any given time. I also sit outside and just sit! I think about what it feels like sitting on the chair, how the chair feels, is the chair supporting my back, is it comfortable? Once I feel at ease then I just listen to what is going on around me. I may hear the neighbour's oil tank running in the winter, the sound of the birds singing in the garden, the rain tapping on the roof and the wind blowing through the trees. I think of the smells, breakfast cooking, the smell of the rain, I do love the smell of the flowers. All these things make me present in the moment.

3. Writing in a Diary

Writing in a diary has helped me throughout my life and I do believe writing in a diary daily really helps me to put things into perspective. Sometimes when I look back at what I have written I am really surprised at how logical it sounds although it may not have been at the time. Writing something down takes it out of your head. Those thoughts that circle in your mind if you are worried about something or if thoughts are just spinning and you can't stop them. Usually when I put them on paper it is out of my head!

4. Journaling

This is different from writing in a diary, this is a Gratitude list. Penning what you are grateful for and celebrating the good things that have happened in your day. Your blessings no matter how small, they are still successes and this releases Serotonin and helps rewire your brain with the good things in your life.

I believe that changing your behaviour for 21 to 30 days becomes a habit. This practice helps to reprogram your brain.

Another part of this process is detailing on paper what you want. Sometimes you might not know what you want, so do what I do, write down what you don't want and the act of doing helps you to see clearer and then what you do want starts to come.

I have done this for years now and now I am able to go out in the morning and verbalise my gratitude list and say aloud what I want and then I thank in advance for what I want as if they have already happened. This really is therapeutic and just taking this time for yourself is so beneficial and again the more you do this habitually the better you feel.

Sometimes I also cut out pictures from magazines to create a mood board of how I see my life in the future. This has previously given me hope and as I mentioned earlier that words have power so do pictures and these pictures help me to visualise the future that I want. Once I make this board I believe that the Law of Attraction is in play and that some of the things have proven to happen. They don't always happen straight away but they have come into being.

I don't want you to think that this is all wishy washy stuff.

These things have become habitual for me as I really did need to practice 'me time' . I rarely gave myself time for myself. Everything I did was for everyone else. So I am not saying that all of the above will definitely help you, it really depends where you are in your own mind set.

Other things I do are maybe much more logical for many of you however I will say don't knock it until you have tried it.

5. Exercise, Exercise, Exercise

Look I hate the very word, however it does work. Any form of physical activity. Walking, Running, Yoga, Pilates, a dance class anything that will get your blood pumping around your body. Of course I am going to mention Singing as it is not just a vocal activity it is also physical when it is done properly and is scientifically proven to be therapeutic. You can get fit singing! Releasing serotonin "the feel good hormone"

I love walking in nature. My favourite is the beach and I regularly drive to Helen's Bay Beach or along Cultra's Beach Road if I want a more peaceful experience. When I need what I call the wind to blow my brains off and knock some sense into me I go to White Rocks Beach in Portrush. Each time I walk along White Rocks I always come away feeling clearer and much, much better.

6. Reiki

What is Reiki?

It is a form of energy healing, from Japan created by Dr Mikao Usui who taught his Reiki System to more than two thousand people in his lifetime. This is a complementary or alternative medicine. Reiki Practitioners use a technique using their hands for healing; the healing is through universal energy transferred through the practitioner's hands. It encourages emotional and/or physical healing.

Reiki I believe has really helped me. If you are like me and you find sleeping a real issue when you are anxious, depressed, and menopausal or just not feeling at yourself then a great benefit of Reiki is getting a deep Reiki Sleep. Need I say more?

These are options to try if you don't feel your usual self however if you do need more support it is essential that you go and see your GP (General Practitioner) just in case you do need other interventions if it is a clinical issue.

7. Breathe

I know it sounds simple, however a daily practice of breathing in and slowing down your breathing will help you to reprogram your breath. Breathe in slowly through your nose and then very slowly breathing out through your mouth two or three cycles of this and then breath in and out through your nose as normal for two or three times and then back to the slow deep inhale through your nose and then the very slow exhale through your mouth. This really will slow your mind down. The more you practice this the better you get and the quicker you can catch the anxiety before it gets to panic mode.

Counselling is great if you just need someone to talk to and go through your personal problems in a safe environment to help you clarify your issues and explore and develop strategies that will help you.

8. CBT – Cognitive Behavioural Therapy

I had CBT and it really did help me. In fact when I returned from London I was referred immediately to CBT Therapy. This therapy helps you to understand that your thoughts, feelings and physical reactions or sensations are interlinked and can easily trap you in a vicious circle.

We can sometimes have unhelpful or unproductive thoughts and CBT helps you to replace these thoughts into more positive thinking. I know that my explanation makes it sound like it is the "Positive Thinking Bullshit" that some have said but it really is much, much more than that. I can confidently say that this therapy was life changing for me.

And finally if it all feels too much like it was for me then you may need to delve a little deeper.

9. Psychotherapy

My understanding of this therapy is that you learn about your condition including your moods, thoughts and behaviours and how your own core beliefs and personality traits have an effect on you.

Tools no. 1 – 7 can be used as a preventative measure in the hope that you never need counselling, CBT, Psychotherapy or even medication. I now use these techniques as a rule of thumb daily.

I now also really trust my intuition and my instinct from the start and trust when something feels right or not. I take each day as it comes and on days where I don't feel good, hour by hour, minute by minute, even, second by second because if I think too far ahead that can cause my anxiety.

I still see 'The Spiritual Life Coach' and 'The Psychotherapist'; it's nothing to be ashamed of. I like to always keep on top of my emotional wellbeing.

Prevention is the key!

ABOUT THE AUTHOR

Author, broadcaster and singing coach Pauline Carville (Post Graduate Diploma R.A.M & BARCS) trained and graduated as a Singer / Singing Teacher from the very prestigious Royal Academy of Music under the mentorship of the renowned Mary Hammond.

She also trained as an Actor at the Royal Conservatoire Scotland. Pauline worked as an Actor/Singer since graduating and has a very successful C.V. having worked with high calibre Directors and Musical Directors including The Royal National Theatre's Trevor Nunn, West End's Matthew Ryan & David White.

Her credits included the Olivier Award Winning Production of Honk the Ugly Duckling, Sweeney Todd and Titanic, Shakespeare's Merchant of Venice & The Comedy of Errors as well as numerous West End concerts and Off Broadway Concerts in NYC.

Pauline also taught Singing & Acting at Redroofs Theatre School, London where she trained up and coming performers including BBC's Danielle Harmer and numerous children from The Harry Potter Movies and West End Musicals.

She has been working as a Singing/Performance Specialist for over 25 years now and continues to develop through personal continual training.

Pauline has trained and mentored many students who have gone on to work in the Music Industry and/or continued their training at Singing & Drama Schools in London including The Royal Academy of Music, Italia Conti Academy, Arts Educational and Mountview where students train in Singing, Musical Theatre or Acting. With regards to Drama school auditions students of Pauline have 100% success rate in gaining places on accredited courses. She works with Professional Singers here in Northern Ireland, Dublin and London.

Pauline has also starred in the movie Post Mortem with Charlie Sheen and has written and appeared in her own one woman show.

Pauline is also a founder Director of Apollo Arts Theatre Company where she Directed the iconic 1980's play Joyriders by Christina Reid and DNA by Dennis Kelly. Both of these productions transferred to The Grand Opera House, Belfast. Her other Directing credits include Willy Russell's Blood Brothers, Chat Room by Enda Walsh and she has produced the musical Chicago, Zombie Prom, Our Day Out and Veronica's Room. In 2019 Pauline was back on stage in the hugely successful panto Aladdin, which she also produced and directed.

Pauline is currently based in Belfast where she continues to run Belfast School Of Singing and Singing Lessons Belfast.

She will soon be launching a Global Singing Coaching side the business aimed at those who have always wanted to s but are stopped by fear, lack of confidence and the gremlin someone telling them they can't sing!

Connect with Pauline

Paulinecarville.com
Instagram: @paulinecarvilleelliott
Facebook: /paulinecarville
Twitter: @CarvillePauline

This book was supported by the
Arts Council of Northern Ireland

artscouncil-ni.org